A Young Man In War

A Young Man In War

VIETNAM PHOENIX ADVISOR
AND A SURVIVOR'S TALE

Paul C. Pritchard

© 2017 Paul C. Pritchard
All rights reserved.

ISBN: 1978398026
ISBN-13: 9781978398023
Library of Congress Control Number: 2017916223
CreateSpace Independent Publishing Platform
North Charleston, South Carolina

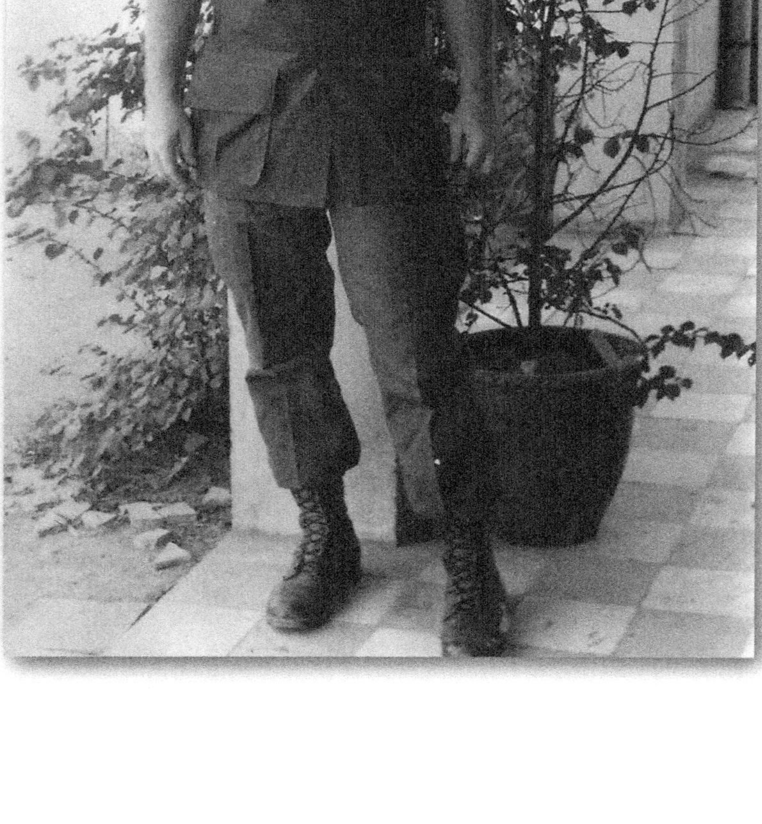

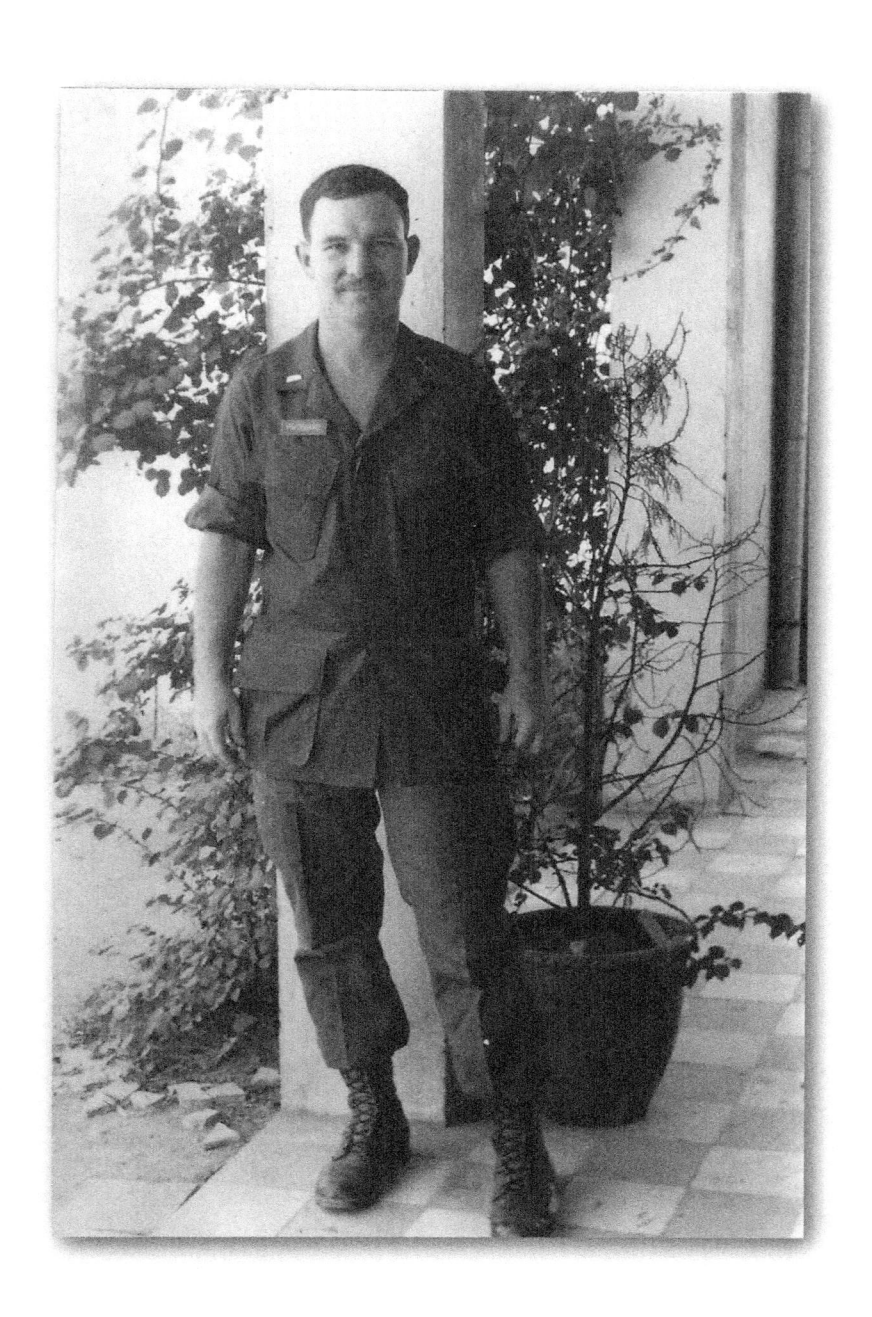

Foreword

⚜

THIS IS A MEMOIR, NOTHING more. The experiences, dates, letters, and locations are as accurate as can be recalled and recorded. The conversations were contrived from actual experiences, often, in truth, me talking to myself. The people are real with fictitious names.

I could not tell everything about my experience, since I avoid trying to recall it. I seldom have seen a movie about Vietnam, except *Apocalypse Now*, which I was told reflected much of my experience. I did not watch the television documentaries about the war, for that matter. I have been diagnosed with PTSD and avoided reading or watching depictions about the war for fear that they might trigger deeper emotions. I still surround myself with pillows at night because I occasionally lash out and fear I might hit my partner. Fortunately, this never stopped me from a wonderful life.

You can tell when people were real American advisors. They went into the swamps, jungles, and forests with their Vietnamese advisees. In my case, the Mekong Delta jungle soup was composed of swamp water and Agent Orange. Periodically I had to go to a hospital in Saigon to have a suction tube put in my ears to suck out the crud. I wish there was such a tube for memories.

Finally, publishing this book was not my idea. I wrote it for myself, beginning October 3, 1987, years ago, to get some things out of the deep caves of my mind and into another container. Now, having written it, I want to thank those who pushed me to get it out.

CHAPTER 1

⚜

IF THERE WAS A BAPTISM in Vietnam, it wasn't by fire. It was from the humid, dusty, sun-dried wash of the helicopters mixed with the sweaty uncertainty of living or dying.

Can Tho airfield was a classic baptismal pool. It was the third stop in two weeks for us. My partner, First Lieutenant John Lippen, and I stood out from those waiting for their helicopters: our new green fatigues, our duffel bags filled with gear that would never be used, our eyes searching for security.

The airfield was the focal point not for combat so much as for the administration of the war for the southern part of South Vietnam. And there was much to administer.

For one thing, everything came in pairs. In the world of being a US Army advisor, for every Vietnamese officer, there was a counterpart American officer. Ostensibly, this was to show that we were there at their request, an ironic invitation to join a war. But I knew, everyone knew, the Vietnamese knew, that the Americans lacked confidence in the ability or the commitment of the Vietnamese to fight and win the war.

In between all of this duplication of two colonels here, two lieutenants there, two sergeants everywhere, were the helicopters, jeeps, phones, desks, and all of the other paraphernalia needed to support one rifle.

The baptism had actually started when I stepped off the plane at Bien Hoa, just outside Saigon, with all the other lieutenants of my class. Before those steps, everything was pretend. ROTC, Fort Sill, Fort Benning, Fort Holabird were the make-believe of becoming an officer. Now it was the real thing. Now it was "Nam."

We spent two too many days in Bien Hoa, one hell of a dirt pile. Then it was into Saigon for everyone to the 525 Military headquarters. That was when I almost saw death jump in front of me and laugh but disappear. It was in the briefing room. There was the sergeant talking about the process of making assignments, the war seen by those in Saigon, the general types of responsibilities we would have. But we already knew everything he was telling us. We had to. Everything in war is a secret to be discovered if you want to survive. Most of the information ferreted out of the administrative clerks and the older officers was 90 percent bullshit, I had found. So it took a lot of input to get the 10 percent that added up to one hundred.

I was ready for this particular briefing. It was exactly what I expected: the old, yellow plaster-walled room, about a hundred chairs, a large board with the outline of Vietnam's provinces, and the pins. The pins were critical. All those 10 percents added up to one conclusion: know where you want to go and then get your name in for the selection of your pin. Each pin identified the assignments:

"I Corps is a conventional war up there," the briefing sergeant said. "Two Corps has a lot of action and needs province advisors. We're here in Three Corps, where some of your buddies will serve in the MACV headquarters. Four Corps is the guerrilla war."

I remembered every detail as I sat in the Can Tho airfield. My first, near-fatal mistake occurred in that briefing room. Then the sergeant told us that we had to get our names on the white slips of paper passed out by the briefing staff and get the names back to the sergeant. So I wrote the fastest I had ever scribbled and got my name back to the sergeant from my front row seat. I had been successful in outsmarting the system. I thought I would get first choice. Then I watched in horror as the sergeant put every slip on top of mine. I would have last choice.

And I did. I got the last pin, duty at Khe Sanh in I Corps, providing army intelligence support for the marines, whom everyone knew were being pounded every night. Khe Sanh was closer to Hanoi than to Saigon. It was in the papers back home. It was the worst assignment. Death was mocking me.

I noticed the way my classmates filed past me, the consoling pats on the shoulder. I knew my chances of survival were one in a hundred.

But then a strange thing happened. A quiet classmate, Lieutenant Peterson, walked up and said, "I wanted to go to the Khe Sanh. Would you be willing to trade before we turn our names in with these pins?"

I didn't even think twice. I didn't even know the assignment Peterson had drawn. But I knew it couldn't be as bad as Khe Sanh, and Peterson's motives were his. Gut response had been a mainstay for me in training.

"No problem," I said. "Let's do it."

Peterson had a Four Corps pin, a place called Sa Dec, which I had never heard of. But that was good. The places I had heard about were notorious. The quiet places were the unknowns. At least, that was what I hoped.

In a daze of disbelief, I walked over to my friend Lippen, or Lip as he was nicknamed, and said, "I got Four Corps."

Lip looked up with his marvelous white-toothed smile and countered, "You son of a bitch, so did I. How did you do that?"

"You'll never believe it," I replied.

The two of us got our names inserted on the cookie-cutter orders that were already typed up, were told when to meet our flight south to Can Tho, and were ready the next day to be closer to someplace instead of "in transit."

We had been in country almost a week now. In Can Tho, a Sergeant First Class Bender picked us up in a jeep at the airfield and took us to the small compound used by the Four Corps intelligence advisory team. The Vietnamese Popular Force guard at the gate was, at best, a joke. He was leaning against the large tree at the entrance, rifle against the wall, grinning as he talked to the Vietnamese women walking out of the compound with their bags of larder. He stopped the jeep on the patio and showed us our quarters, a room with no windows. "Lunch is down the hall, sirs." Then he left to get back to his jeep. Bender had a coveted job, I guessed. He had a jeep and the freedom to go and do as he pleased. I stood on the old second-story porch, watching him drive away into the diesel-choked air of the broad, tree-lined street crowded with too many vehicles.

As I watched him disappear, I realized that he and I were both here looking for ourselves. He had a jeep, freedom, a job. He seemed in control of his life. I was in control but still very early in the journey. I had not fought assignment to Vietnam like most of my classmates. Nor did I volunteer. It was more of a duty. My father had done his duty; so had my brother. I still had the rifle my great grandfather used in the Civil War.

I didn't consider myself a fighter. But this war was an enigma to me. At home, it was right to some and wrong to others. It was a "domino theory," a "conflict" rather than a war.

Whatever it was, it was not something I felt was clearly wrong. I felt I had to experience this war, the war of my generation, the war nobody claimed. Cowardice was wrong, no matter what others called it.

I had committed myself to face it and survive it. And the prospect of facing it and surviving pulled me into each day, into each experience.

I walked back to my room, where I found Lip writing to Marsha, his wife of but one month. Lip looked up with a gentle smile.

"Three hundred and fifty-nine more days, ole buddy," he offered.

While I was living for the experience here, he relished his return.

"You know, it will be a month before I hear from her. But I'm going to keep the letters going, one a day, if it kills me."

Then he pulled out the photo of her taken on their honeymoon. She was beautiful with long, straight, black hair in the sixties style. I had been the best man—a surprising honor, I felt, since Lip and I had barely known each other before February, when we met in infantry officers basic at Fort Benning. We grew to enjoy each other's company like two vibrant paints balancing each other on a canvas.

As Lip wrote, I thought about home and the life awaiting me. There was no wife like Marsha for me. I liked Libba, whom I had just met during the time I had spent at Fort Holabird. She was also from the South. Her brilliance and smile were appealing to a boy from the plains side of Kansas City. But I really didn't know her. We were both under the influence of so many other forces: I, going to war; she, going to work, both trying to please each other. Then I flew here. To Nam.

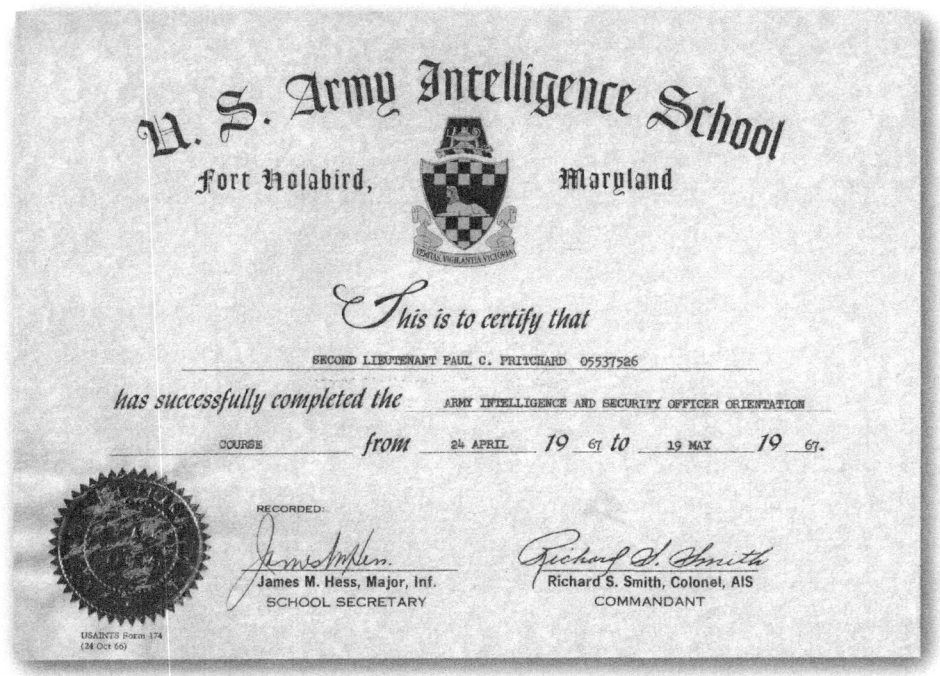

U.S. Army Intelligence School Graduation Certificate

    My thoughts were interrupted by people walking along the corridor. There was a brief introductory knock on the door, and then a head stuck in.

    "You're Lippen and Pritchard, right? My name is Kress." The greeting was casual, as the military-intelligence types tended to be. "I'm here to brief you before you head up to Sa Dec. Let's have lunch."

    Lip had his letter put away and was in step with Kress almost as fast as I was. The corridor, as the noise had indicated to me, was the main artery to the dining room. It was a large room, glassed in on one side, with wooden chairs lining six tables. There was no formality. We sat down without regard for rank, and the same food was brought to everyone by a Vietnamese staff person. It was much like my fraternity. The few seniors who isolated themselves at one table were much like the field grade officers who had one table nicely tucked in the corner. Nothing else. The rest of the men, regardless of rank, sat in the first open seat they felt comfortable in.

Three young sergeants, who looked like us three lieutenants, sat across from us at the table.

"Are we playing tonight?" one asked Kress.

"At five," Kress responded after a long drink of iced tea.

The sugar came in a very large granule form and had a brown tint to it. Kress had put about one inch of the slowly dissolving crystals on the bottom of his tea glass before he drank it down.

"Who are we playing?" the sergeant asked.

"The transportation guys again. I hope they bring out their cheerleaders. They were a gas." Kress turned to us and explained, "The other team paid some of the local bar girls to come out for the volleyball game dressed in bikinis with pom-poms. You should hear 'Sis-boom-bah' in a Vietnamese accent." Then turning to the sergeant, he introduced us. "Lane, Jerves, Peterson, meet Pritchard and Lippen. New in country heading for the Ninth ARVN. These guys run the photo lab. Where did you guys go to school?" He turned his head to look at us, the ones being addressed.

I was the one without food in his mouth, "University of Missouri," I replied.

Lip picked up, adding, "Ole Miss. I was teaching there. That's why I was bestowed with my nickname."

Kress smiled, then described the collegiate backgrounds to the three NCOs across the table. It was clear why rank was inconsequential here. As I looked around, I concluded that everyone probably was a college graduate and that role and function seemed to determine relationships, not rank.

The Vietnamese staff kept the food coming and the used dishes going. They wasted no energy with their shuffle walk. Kress got up first after everyone was finished.

"Let's get into the briefing."

We left our tablemates who were thinking of how to rival the cheerleaders and walked through a corridor of the old French colonial building, down the wide steps, and through two other rooms. Finally, we were in what was clearly the official briefing room. A map of South Vietnam was on one wall, about eight feet high, mirrored by a second map of the same dimensions showing just the Four Corps area.

"Sit down," Kress said, pulling out a retractable pointer from his pocket. "I'm going to bring you up to date on our situation here in the Four Corps. We've got our own war here. When you get to Sa Dec, you will hear more about the Ninth ARVN's provinces. As you can see, we run from the Cambodian border along the Mekong River, south to the South China Sea. We have the U Minh Forest, the Plain of Reeds here, and the Three Sisters Mountains on the Cambodian border. Those are the centers of conflict, where Charlie likes to concentrate. We suspect they are also coming into the Run Sat, this large swamp south of Saigon. It's out of our area, but they may be using our provinces here to supply food and keep their families. We have reports of periodic troop concentrations here." His pointer was a second or two behind his comments, reinforcing his conclusions.

"Specifically, you are both being assigned to the Ninetieth Advisory Team here at Sa Dec. You may be reassigned within the provinces of the division's area of operation. Colonel Bough is the ranking advisor. He has just come in country.

"The Ninth ARVN Division is OK: slow to respond but good at keeping things quiet. They are not the crack division that the Seventh ARVN is." Kress continued, explaining the sizes of the Army of the Republic of Vietnam units we supported and the equipment that we had supplied. I tried to mentally record it but found the facts overwhelming and more scholarly than essential to my needs. I watched Kress as he casually used the pointer to describe the history of the war from his perspective in Can Tho.

"We're fighting a classic guerrilla conflict here, unlike the other corps," Kress said. "The Viet Cong like to catch us off guard in the provinces: mortar at night, ambush or sniper during the day. Mines are everywhere. Watch your step. Charlie will hit when you least suspect."

Kress said in summary, "Our mission is to support and advise the commanding officer of the Ninth ARVN, Lieutenant General Kwan. You work through Colonel Bough, a very impressive guy who was a classmate of Westmoreland's at the Point."

Colored pins on the board concentrated in a few areas. When Kress asked for questions, Lip responded, "What do the pins mean?"

Kress described the events of the previous night and the briefing that had been given that morning for the US colonel commanding the advisors and his Vietnamese counterpart.

"Sa Dec reports in each morning on the status of the night's operations, KIAs, prisoners, and other strategic information from all of their provinces. We also get it from the other Vietnamese division advisors and prepare a corps briefing here. These yellow pins were mortar attacks at outposts and other sites. There were a few sightings of small troop movements by SLAR—you know, side-looking airborne radar craft shown in red—and no contact with a sweep operation here in Hoa Hao. We lost four ARVN in all of this and got twenty VC KIAs and approximately fifty VC wounded."

Kress then looked at us, paused, and said with a sense of frustration, "If you believe that, I've got a bridge in New York I want you to buy. But we pass this bullshit on to Saigon."

"How do you know it's bullshit?" I asked.

"Experience."

Lip moved us back to our future. "What's the Ninth ARVN like? I mean, the town. Is it VC?"

Kress responded quickly, "I don't know. I've only been there once to visit the unit. I like it here, and I've spent my ten months right here in Can Tho."

His comments reminded me of previous briefings. The men in Saigon had never been to Can Tho. In Benning, a few of the training staff had been in Vietnam. Most had come from Germany. It was standard procedure that whoever briefed about something or someplace had never done it or been there.

Kress broke our silence. "I've got sixty days in country, guys. I don't want to read about you as a statistic. Don't volunteer. Follow the lesson and you won't go out in a body bag."

We sat in the airfield staging building, and I recounted vividly all of the events of the past days. Next to me, Lip was lost in another letter.

I strolled out of the doors and looked at the array of planes with technicians, vehicles, and crews scurrying around the Can Tho airfield. There were a couple of craft with side-looking airborne radar, the SLAR, that we had been taught could pick up a water buffalo or two sampans moving after curfew. The helicopters seemed worn. There were a few of the newer models, bigger, shinier. Dust clouds picked up from the wash of the helicopter rotors.

Technology was the cause of this war, one of my friends had said. "They got all these new weapons, and they want to test them out." His sarcastic add-on, "And we get to test them," gave me a sense of my worth.

I walked back in, sat on the wooden bench with my back to the wall, facing all the others who were waiting, in transit, and closed my eyes. The rotating fans overhead kept the air moving. *Better than the chopper's wash from the rotors*, I thought. But the sweat rolled down my skin. *Baptism*, I thought.

"Lieutenant Pritchard! Lieutenant Lippin!" A sergeant with a clipboard yelled through the door.

"Here!" we responded.

"Time to mount up."

Then the sergeant disappeared like so many others who seemed to control the direction of my life.

CHAPTER 2

⚜

FROM THE MOMENT OF OUR arrival, I thought that Sa Dec was a bunch of contradictions. First, Sa Dec was a concentration of military activity in a compound on a triangle of land surrounded by two canals and the town. It was an easy target.

View of the Sa Dec residents' homes across the canal

Everything that I had learned and everything that I felt essential to my survival seemed to be compromised in Sa Dec.

I had been assigned to a different hooch than Lip. Each hooch housed about eight men in a space about fourteen feet wide and twenty feet long. Each man had a bunk, a standing metal locker, and a small space with a desk and chair. The major storage was under the bunk.

The hooch reminded me of a Boy Scout cabin, except its exterior walls were metal rather than canvas from the ground up to about four feet. But both had screen to the roof line. The roof overhang was necessary when the monsoon rains came.

Surrounding each hooch, like silent sentries, were fifty-five-gallon metal containers filled with sand. These were for mortar protection. Unfortunately, when the compound had been built, the settling had not occurred. Heavy monsoon runoff from the roof filled in a kind of makeshift moat around each of the hooches. You had to wade through it. (That is, provided that the mortar wasn't a direct hit, in which case it would take out eight men.)

It was another contradiction, but I should not have been surprised. The US military had built unprotected buildings in the classical "wrong" place in the wrong way.

With the town on all three sides, a perfect crossfire could be set up across the water from the civilian huts that lined the water's edge.

But that was not the only mistake of the site, I found. "Hey, we get mortared all the time!" I was told in the bar hooch one night. Lieutenant Jim Drake had been at Sa Dec for about forty-five days and had enough experience to feel he was a veteran. He joked about the mortars. "You see, Charlie just jumps out of the bushes on any of the straight-line roads that radiate from the compound here, drops his mortar tube at a good angle, and fires off a round or two. So they hit in the water. Nobody sleeps for the rest of the night. And if he hits, well, we're so packed in here, one good round in one hooch would blow away eight men."

The other contradictions were psychological as well as physical.

Two days had passed since Lip and I had arrived in Sa Dec. The first was full of the official greetings and getting to know the other officers. The second was a more intensive day of discussions about the status of the G2 operations by another captain, Jack Williams. Williams and Major LaRue, the senior intelligence advisor, had both come in from service in Germany during the past two months and were themselves getting oriented. They were both products of the old school of intelligence with many technical skills such as language and photo interpretive training. Occasionally, one would joke in German and the other would respond.

It suited Lip perfectly. His PhD was in English literature, twelfth and thirteenth centuries, and his language was classical German. I was always a little at the edge of their conversations. Lip and I were told on the second day that one of us would be staying in Sa Dec and one would go to the province of Vinh Long to be the intelligence officer for the advisors there. As I watched the camaraderie develop among the three of them, I grew to accept the fate of heading down river to the other assignment.

In a way, I could justify the inevitability of that decision. My job at Sa Dec would have been to work in all of the provinces, including Vinh Long, handing out the intelligence support funds, serving on rotation as the reconnaissance company advisory, and being the G2 briefer on his day off field duty.

"Vinh Long," Williams told me, "has a good advisory team, although there are only ten Americans compared to the sixty here at Sa Dec. The town is fairly quiet. It has the main airfield and American pilots flying support for the corps. In short, it's a good place to be a field advisory and learn the war."

On day three, Lip was already at breakfast when I came in. He was talking with two other officers from his hooch. I joined them for the usual fare of scrambled eggs made out of the powdered facsimile, coffee, and juice.

"Captain Williams just told me that I've got the briefing tomorrow," Lip said.

He was pleased as I would be. My fate was again cast. I had missed this casual meeting with Williams at breakfast. It wasn't scheduled, but it seemed fortuitous for Lip.

We finished our breakfast and walked across the dirt street that separated the mess hall from the old French stucco headquarters.

"Good morning, gentlemen," we heard from behind. It was Colonel Bough, the senior advisor. He made an immediate impression with a tall figure, silver hair, and a warm smile. "I understand you two are joining us."

"Yes, sir," I said, "we've been here for three days working with Major LaRue."

"Well, we're glad you're here. I'm sure I'll be seeing more of you." We saluted as he walked off up the wide, covered stairs of the old provincial headquarters building.

"He was just up with Westmoreland," Lip said. "Something about a major offensive. I heard it from Captain Baker at breakfast."

Behind again, I thought.

When we got to the G2 office, Major LaRue was talking through an interpreter with his counterpart, Major Ho. The interpreter was slow and searching for the correct word, his grammar very basic. We walked past the attempted bilingual conversation to the opposite end of the room and into the office of Captain Williams.

"Good morning, Lieutenant Pritchard. You'll be working with the interrogation team today. The ARVN brought in some prisoners last night. Lieutenant Lippen, this morning you will observe the general's briefing and then have duty tonight before you give the briefing tomorrow morning."

Captain Williams looked tired from his turn at staying up in the operation room all night. He had changed his uniform this morning for the briefing, but the strain was visible in his circled eyes.

"Pritchard, I want you to meet Trung We Wa, the chief of the interrogation team. You will be with him as observer."

One of the Vietnamese Officers and his family

"Welcome, Te We," the thin and grinning Vietnamese first lieutenant offered in English, noting my second lieutenant rank. "How long you in Vietnam?"

We walked out of the office and down the wide steps exchanging the usual pleasantries. "Yes, Vietnam was very beautiful; yes, the weather was hot."

His five-foot, six-inch height belied his superiority in this world. He spoke English and was already assessing this new American.

For once, though, I was relaxed, already reconciled to moving to Vinh Long, which sure beat Khe Sanh, I mused.

Across the narrow street from the headquarters building was a gate in the four-foot-high stucco wall. On the other side of the wall was the maze of low buildings that housed the soldiers of the Vietnamese generals' staff. We walked through the gate.

Pleasantries evaporated as Wa suddenly turned serious.

"First time you see interrogation. Not very nice. VC not nice either. We catch VC last night on road. We think they mortar attack."

We walked toward a group of sloppily dressed Vietnamese enlisted men who were standing outside one of the metal buildings. The men cleared a path as we headed into the building.

Inside was a young girl, hands tied behind her back, kneeling on the floor. She looked strained, sweat pouring from her forehead. One of the enlisted men held an electric wire connected to a battery to her exposed foot.

My stomach knotted.

The questions flew at her. Each question brought the same head shake of denial from her and the same demand from the interrogator coupled with a brief electric jolt.

I tapped my counterpart on the shoulder, gesturing toward the door.

I had absolutely no idea how to stop this, but my first instinct was to do so. My second instinct told me that doing so could spell my doom on this first assignment. But I spoke from my wrenching gut.

"Trung We, can't do. We can't shock prisoners. I must tell the major. He will tell the colonel. The colonel will tell the general and the US generals in Saigon."

Once meaningless, the fine print of the Geneva Conventions for prisoner treatment floated about in my head. They gave substance to my concern for another life and maybe mine. Wa gazed quizzically at me. He was surprised at my quick reaction, and I wondered if he would do what I wanted. Then my instinct saved me.

"Trung We, if story gets to Saigon and US generals know of this, the US news reporters will know. Soon, US television come to Sa Dec. And they make movie for all American people to see torture. Then American people will tell US Congress to stop money and supplies."

This, apparently made sense. Without hesitating, Wa shouted a command. We walked back in. The wire was put aside. The interrogator continued to yell out his questions. The prisoner continued her denials. Nothing seemed to transpire, except that her body seemed to relax with the respite from the shocks. The spectators still watched, and I served as sentry over this one life in jeopardy.

Soon, we walked outside. Wa offered me a cigarette. The heat inside the building had left me soaked and depleted. I accepted the cigarette as a courtesy. Until then, I didn't smoke cigarettes.

"I like you," Wa said simply. "You know television people in USA. You have lunch with me in Sa Dec."

It was a small victory for that moment. I had stopped the torture, even for a short while, and my counterpart seemed to respect the power. Power being everything, everywhere, especially in the Orient, I played the card again.

"Yes, I was a reporter for a newspaper. I know press. Maybe I can make you a hero." I smiled. I had been a reporter for the Kansas City STAR and in fact did write a lengthy story about a returning veteran. The GI later told me his friends called him a "hero."

Wa smiled, cigarette smoke streaming from between his teeth. "Yes, yes! I like."

When I got back to the office, Captain Williams was finishing up some paperwork and invited me to lunch.

"Well, Pritchard, how did it go?"

I told him what had happened. Except the part about getting into the public relations business in Sa Dec.

"Do you think you stopped it?" he asked.

"I hope so," I said truthfully.

The afternoon was filled with discussions about the management of intelligence funds used to pay informers. That was the captain's main interest, it seemed. He was "career."

Throughout the discussions, the tension was subtly apparent between Lip and me. We both wished that the decision would be made about who was heading south and who was staying. I think we both wanted the uncertainty to stop, to just be someplace, to be at home, whatever that meant in a war zone.

That evening was the first in many that Lip and I were not together. The brief days at Sa Dec were quickly pulling us apart. Lip was on duty that night. I spent an hour in the club, then headed back to my hooch to write a letter home. I had hoped to be able to tell my parents what my address was going to be. I knew that it would be a month from whenever I told them where I was until I would hear from them. The letter was the brief, all-is-well, I-am-with-good-people, they-should-not-worry, how-is-home report. It was to reassure them. But it didn't reassure me.

Breakfast the next morning was a welcomed relief from a hot and sleepless night under the mosquito netting of my bunk. I wanted to observe Lip's briefing.

He emerged from his hooch, having changed into a fresh uniform that still showed the creases of his duffel bag. He looked better than I felt.

"How did it go?" I asked.

"Old friend, I kept the war down to a dull roar," he responded.

We walked up to the second-floor briefing room. After all the senior staff of US and Vietnamese officers filled the ten or so chairs of the briefing room, the Vietnamese general walked in with Colonel Bough. Compared to the colonel, the general looked young, but he moved with an assurance that left no doubt that he was well aware of his importance. He sat; Bough sat. Then we sat.

The Official Photo of the U.S. Advisory Team at Sa Dec
Lt. Pritchard front row, second from right

"Good morning, General, Colonel. It is July 31. Time check is 7:03." Lip began in the time-honored tradition of the morning briefing.

Pointing to the large board, Lip quickly began reviewing the symbols of the prior night's action on the board. He stopped with the sound of murmurs from the room.

A Vietnamese major, sitting behind the general, leaned forward quietly discussing something with the general, apparently about one of the sites Lip had described. Colonel Bough glanced at Lip and turned to the general and the major to make sure they were through.

"Please continue, Lieutenant."

Lip did. He moved from the past to the present.

"Today's weather will be…"

"Lieutenant, today's weather is like every other day's weather in this season," Colonel Bough interrupted, but gently. "Thank you."

There were smiles, but it was a fairly pleasant dismissal and without embarrassment for Lip.

I was impressed and rather relieved, actually. Lip would enjoy this assignment if I were the one to go to Vinh Long. I, on the other hand, was not excited about being on stage.

"Good going, Lip," I said as he joined me in the back of the room.

Lip agreed and smiled.

The briefing continued with another US advisor, now covering plans for troop actions for the day. There were occasional interruptions as the general discussed a point with his senior staff.

When the briefing was over, the general rose. All stood at attention as the general and Colonel Bough walked out. Lip headed off to sleep, and I walked back into the G2 office as the others filtered out to their respective jobs.

Major LaRue was in the office and gestured to me.

"Lieutenant, please join me. I understand that you speak French."

"The traditional college version, sir," I responded.

"Well, let's give it a try this morning. Our interpreter is out, and I need your help."

Give it a try was about right. My last French class was in my sophomore year at the University of Missouri. I took it to pass a requirement for my BA, not to survive in a war.

Our Vietnamese major walked in to a chorus of welcomes in Vietnamese from the administrative staff in the front room. Major LaRue also welcomed him, though in English.

"Te We speaks French, Dai We. He will be our interpreter." LaRue looked at me expectantly.

"Bon matin, Dai We."

Easy. Now I had to create sentences out of a foreign language for thoughts I had never experienced.

"Ma francais es tres malheureuse. S'il vous plaît, parlez lentement." I appealed to him to excuse my lack of ability and speak slowly.

The major smiled.

"Tres bien," he began, "Te We est tres intelligent. Mais, c'est possible pour vous a faire mon lieutenant un hero?" Word travelled fast, and Tung We had obviously been broadcasting my offer. The major smiled with his joke.

LaRue smiled at our rapport. I explained our joke. *Humor binds our diversity*, I thought.

Major LaRue asked me to explain that he was on his way to Saigon for a meeting on a new type of aircraft and that he would return to brief the major. LaRue wondered if there was anything he could bring the major from Saigon. There were a few more thoughts.

I did my best.

The major listened and smiled. I sensed he understood much of LaRue's English. He said that he needed nothing.

After a few more formalities, the major left. LaRue thanked me. I was about to leave when Captain Williams stopped me.

"You did well. The Dai We seemed happy to have someone who can converse with him. You know, there are a lot of Vietnamese officers who can speak French, and they don't care about speaking English," Williams mused. "Pritchard, you know, LaRue and the colonel liked what you did in that interrogation. Irregular, but they liked it." Then parenthetically, he added, "You're staying at Sa Dec."

I was floored, surprised, amazed, excited, happy, and most of all, relieved.

Lunch brought the news to Lip. I wondered how he would take it. He joined Captain Williams and me at the table, and Williams mentioned it rather casually. Lip was obviously surprised but still ready for war, solemn and accepting.

"When do I head out?" he asked.

"As soon as we have a convoy heading there. You should plan on the one tomorrow if there are no changes."

Lip finished his lunch in still-sleepy silence and headed back to bed.

I found Lip later that afternoon, not in his hooch as I had expected, but in the bar, talking with another officer.

"What exactly did you do, ole buddy?" he asked.

"I was surprised, too," I shrugged, ordering my beer.

LaRue was sitting at a table across the room, and I moved in that direction. "May I join you?" I asked.

"Certainly, Lieutenant. Welcome to Sa Dec."

Welcome to Sa Dec indeed. And goodbye, it seemed, to a friend.

Dear Brenda and Gang,

A thousand congratulations on the birth of Andy. From all the praise that I have heard about this little fellow, I can't wait to see him. The only news that compared with it was the word that Doc and Annie are counting the months. The way things are going and growing, I may be a grand uncle before I make you all aunts and uncles.

The rainy season is upon us, so the weather is fairly pleasant here in the delta. The sampans and tree-trunk boats are putting up and down the river. The paddies are covered with standing water and silt to make the rice crop fertile and their work productive. It is really a sight to see. But, in a few months, the metamorphosis will occur, and the delta will all but dry up. The winds will come from the opposite direction with the dry gusts that spell the dry season.

Today, I took a chopper to Rach Gia (Rock Jaw) to visit with our people over there and to deliver some money. The town is really very nice. The town rests on the banks of the Gulf of Thailand and enjoys its pleasant breezes and the fruits of the sea such as shrimp about the size of your hand. It is interlaced with parks and colorful pagodas that are lovely to see.

But with my trip to Rach Gia, I missed out on seeing Premier Ky, who came to Sa Dec today. I left just as he arrived. Fortunately, some of my friends were there and got some pictures of him. That's the breaks of being a peon and a need for someone to go out from the intelligence shop.

With that, I shall close. Keep that little man for me, Johnnie and Susu. I'm counting on you two to be the best helpers you can for your mom and dad.

Love,
Paul

CHAPTER 3

⚜

My days at Sa Dec quickly slid into the routines of war.

The first permanent bunk available was one of another lieutenant who was recovering in Saigon from a wound. Soon he would be rotating back to the States.

It was a good bunk for one reason only. It was the closest to the mortar bunker. On several nights, it was good to be the first one out of bed when incoming rounds started dropping into the surrounding area.

Lucky 7 is the club at the end of the compound lane for all the advisory team

I had skipped lunch one day and had walked down to the patrol boat river (PBR) dock that the navy used. I was chatting with the crew about the locations where they had been picking up machine gun fire along the Mekong. Suddenly, my interpreter, Private Le, came running and shouting down the dirt road.

That caught my attention. It was unusual to see Le move that fast, though he occasionally geared up to a lazy sort of running gait.

"Te We must come to headquarters!" he yelled, running and waving at me. "Captain Weiner in trouble! Te We must come!"

Weiner had field duty with the reconnaissance company that day. One of the G2 junior officers and an NCO, usually Sergeant Litzenger, would go with the thirty-man company. But enemy contact was seldom, and then usually a two or three VC in a sampan, I had found. They had left early in the morning by chopper and were not expected back before sunset. It was a routine search operation and no one expected very much from it. For the Ninth Vietnamese division, the routine was to avoid contact.

I ran back to the headquarters building with Le trailing behind me. The operations center was crowded as I entered, full of US and ARVN officers. The general was absent, but none of his senior officers seemed to be. Colonel Bough was on the mike talking to the US lieutenant colonel who advised the Sa Dec province troops.

"Turnage, see if you can give them cover so we can get Weiner out. We'll send in Pritchard. Over."

"Wilco!" came Turnage's response from the mike. "What's Pritchard's ETA? Over."

I knew Turnage only slightly. In fact, all I knew was that he was always accurate with his jargon and he never seemed to relax. His province was one of seven under our division, an area like a large county.

The desk officer handling the incoming chopper yelled out to the colonel, "Fifteen minutes before she's here, sir. We'll have Pritchard there in another twenty."

Bough relayed the answer to Turnage and the radio communication continued.

LaRue approached me, "Weiner may have been hit, Pritchard. The company is taking fire. You're going in when we take Red out. Get your gear."

I didn't like the sound of this. But after a month, I was ready and confident that I could handle it.

As I ran back to my hooch, Private Le was not far behind me.

"Te We! Te We!" he began, "this time I not go, OK?" It was less a query than a plea. "Captain Weiner interpreter, he be with you. I stay here. Go next time. OK?"

I was too busy packing up to look at him, but I sympathized. Le was an artist, not a soldier, and he knew it wouldn't take much to convince me.

"OK, Le, you paint a picture for me."

"Good deal, Te We!" Le responded with a big smile. "I go paint later. But now I listen so you be safe."

Le was a very good oil painter. I had seen some of his work and had even written home to Kansas City to get him the kind of canvas he needed. I had been to Le's small, one-room apartment in Sa Dec, which was filled with his paintings. He used every conceivable thing on which to paint. His paintings covered every inch of wall space and even hung from coat hangers suspended above his bed. He was a gentle young man and a quick friend. He asked for nothing except the understanding that he not be asked to do those acts he abhorred. Like war.

Alone again, I continued the ritual preparations I had grown accustomed to performing. I tucked the bottom of my trousers into the top of my boots, then covered the interface with masking tape. It helped keep out the leeches, I had learned, and it was better than the duct tape that some guys used that reflected light. So I used masking tape borrowed from the administration office. It didn't reflect, but it only lasted for a day in the paddy water.

I slid my belt halfway out and put the small derringer holster on the belt so that the pistol rode in the middle of my back. The pistol was an unexpected gift from a departing officer. He told me he had never used it. I hoped I would never either, but I found a kind of comfort and security in it since it was the last resort if I were captured, I thought.

The ceremony continued. I was getting better and faster at it. It was the same routine for each mission, and this was my seventh.

The first one had been memorable and embarrassing. I ran out of my hooch that day in an excess of caution in a flak jacket and steel helmet. I was greeted with chuckles from the Vietnamese. They traveled light in the sweltering heat. The "steel pot" afforded me no sun protection, and I soon sported quite a sunburn.

Steel Pot and full battle equipment

Since that first lesson, I wore as little as they did, including a soft Nam hat with a brim. That way, the only things that made me obvious to the VC as an advisor were my five or so inches of height above the line of the Vietnamese soldiers and my bulk of about 165 pounds compared to their average hundred pounds.

I pulled out my M16, added a canvas-covered canteen to my waist belt, and checked the ammunition clips in the pouch that hung from my shoulder suspenders and hooked onto my belt.

The last of my ritual was essential, I had learned. I took my wallet out of my pocket and took off my watch. Litzenger taught me that it was always best to leave valuables behind. No rings, nothing of value.

I could hear the chopper coming as I ran down the road to the pad. It was out of Vinh Long airfield, an old Bravo model. Someone with a sense of humor had carefully placed a Delta Airlines bumper sticker on the chopper's side between the pilot's door and the passenger area.

"Ready when you are!"

The door gunner was young; the pilot, a lieutenant. I didn't know them but had seen them before. I jumped in the open door, with the copilot watching to make sure I fastened the seatbelt, and we lifted off. "Safety first," he joked. *Irony is the common language of war*, I thought.

Despite all the noise, I watched the clouds. They were beginning to grow full with the monsoon rains. Not a bit like September in Kansas City. Nam had two seasons, and that disoriented me. It was either dry or wet, or not far in between. But it was always hot, and I seemed to sweat just as much in the dry season as in the wet. Clouds were calm, each unique, seldom thrusting. They were also changing so that there was always drama. And it was cool up in the clouds.

Suddenly, I returned to reality as the pilot turned to me, pointing to the landing site. He knew the rotor noise would drown out his words. And I knew his thoughts. We circled for several minutes as gunships strafed the site. Then the pilot headed in.

Weiner was standing in the trees by a wet paddy as the chopper landed. He had a bandage on his upper right arm and was helped to the chopper door by Sergeant Litzenger. I watched as they approached.

The wound was superficial. There was only a small spot of blood on the white gauze. But it was clear that Weiner needed to get out. He was shaking, sweating, eyes only on the chopper, consumed with safety, with escape. He was in some kind of shock. I offered him a hand. He took it, without a word, his eyes always on the chopper.

As fast as Weiner hit the floor of the chopper, it pulled out. The door gunners aimed in the trees and cut loose a few rounds in goodbye.

I followed Litzenger to the row of trees that surrounded the paddy. The Vietnamese reconnaissance company was on the ground, covering both directions of possible fire. No one else was wounded. Captain An was talking on the radio in Vietnamese.

I turned to Litzenger, and he read the question in my eyes.

"Weiner is out of it, Lieutenant. We've taken fire all morning, and they were all aiming for Weiner and me. He knew it. The last time we started taking some sniper fire, he hit the ground. That's how he got the wound. Just a graze, but he's in shock. I guess from fear."

"Where are they?" I asked, looking around.

"The last we saw of them, they were right where those two tree lines meet. I don't know...the gunships either got them or they moved out."

If I had to be there, I was glad it was with Litzenger and not Weiner. Litzenger was a staff sergeant, a solid professional. He had been in country for ten years and lived in Sa Dec with his Vietnamese wife. I had heard that he had been a sergeant major in Saigon in charge of one of the NCO clubs, but he got caught up in the khaki Cosa Nostra, which was still getting press in the States. NCOs taking bribes from contractors and suppliers of Saigon's clubs was good copy for the US press. Anyway, I found him dependable.

Litzenger was carrying an M16, and that didn't ease my mind a bit. He usually carried only our radio and a silver .45. The first time I went out on a mission with him, I asked where his rifle was.

"If there's serious action, I'll have one," he had said. Now, there it was.

Captain An signed off his radio and shouted the *laida* command to his troops to assemble. They all rose and began moving cautiously in the direction of the last sighting of the VC.

"Where are the VC, Captain?" I asked in French.

He replied in a rapid French contraction, "I don't know."

Captain An was thin and grizzled. He had seen a lot of action with the French. He still wore his burgundy beret and prided himself in speaking French. He always flashed me a brief smile, pleased that I could speak his second language, his language of war.

He walked, and I followed. He seemed puzzled by something.

"Beaucoup, beaucoup," he muttered to me, "beaucoup VC."

His thirty or so ARVN troops proceeded cautiously in single file. Each man was watching to his side and at the same time down to the spot where he would put his next step. They were crack troops. Captain An chose his men personally. He had survived a lot of firefights because of it. And he had survived a lot of political fights because of it, too. Even though his job was to make contact with Charlie, he lost few men.

When we came within about a hundred yards of the spot where the VC had been, I could see the downed trees and small fires caused by the gunship weapons. I had smelled the smoke and the gunpowder when we landed, and it grew in intensity with every step.

We stopped as we reached the site, and Captain An was immediately back on his radio, reporting our status.

I kept quiet. My job was to advise when needed. With Captain An, the needs weren't many.

The troops moved around Captain An and me, heading for the area that was smoking. The smells increased with a waft of a breeze. They were walking low, ready for fire. None came.

Captain An, Litzenger, and I moved up for the inspection.

The VC had dug in, obviously planning for a serious fight. They had not counted on the gunships coming in so fast or so accurately. One of the grenade-type rounds from the gunship had blown up in a bunker. There were body parts, clotting blood on fragments of black fabric, part of a head.

One VC rifle, an old single-shot MAS, lay on the ground still pointed in the direction of the spot where my chopper had landed. It never ceased to amaze me that the VC would carry this particular rifle, which was almost as long as they were tall.

Captain An stooped over something, picked it up, and turned to me. His look was no longer puzzled. It was clearly troubled. He showed me.

In his hand were cartridges that had been half buried. They were not the hand-packed rounds like the MAS or the Chicom rifles of World War II. They were AK-47 shells. The AK-47, an automatic rifle, was used only by the best Viet Cong troops. From what I had seen, the AK-47s were better than our new M16 rifles. Now I understood. Captain An had sensed that something was wrong, something was out of place. It was probably the sound. Every rifle makes its own kind of noise to a soldier. Each military unit had its own kind of sound, the cacophony and tone of the types of weaponry it carried. This VC unit must have been new to him.

He spoke to me in French, his tone grave.

"These VC have the AK-47 automatic rifles. Here is the proof. We have not seen these before. I must tell Division."

I agreed and told him we would tell my colonel. An's men carried carbines. The war was escalating. But the real question was why.

Captain An spoke quickly into his radio in Vietnamese, translating his message into code without effort. He seemed to be finishing before Litzenger could even start to encode the message he would send.

"How can we get the word back quickly to alert the others without letting Charlie know we know he has the AK-47s? We've got to tell them, and An's almost ready to move out!"

Litzenger, still half listening to Captain An, looked at me.

"Wait one."

Then Litzenger was on the radio.

"Babyface, this is Big Boy. Over."

"Go ahead, Big Boy. Over."

"Babyface, they've upped the ante. We got ourselves a bunch of Al Capones, Babyface, with the new Thompsons."

Litzenger finished, and there was silence. Obviously, somebody was trying to decipher his message. It certainly was irregular but just like him. I could picture the head scratching back at headquarters until it dawned on them that it wasn't code but rather just Litzenger reaching to his years of real experience and using words only an American could interpret. We waited. Captain An continued to talk on his radio.

"Roger, Big Boy. We copy. Out." The headquarters response was abrupt but correct. It was the operations officer, not the colonel. But I could picture the colonel, now probably gathering his staff to discuss this new reality of the war, that they were professional troops, that he hoped they didn't know that we knew.

As Litzenger talked, I listed to An.

"More bad news, Sergeant," I said. "An says we've got a large group of VC, and we're going to follow."

So this was it. My missions so far had been light, more like the Boy Scout hikes I used to take back in Kansas City. I had never been in contact with a large group of VC, just small skirmishes.

The Vietnamese troops were digging, looking for buried weapons. They reassembled without finding anything. But the weapons were there, waiting for the future need.

I felt my senses sharpen, suddenly aware of a smell. It took me a moment to realize what it was. More than smoke or gunpowder, the smell had to be burning flesh.

CHAPTER 4

❧

CAPTAIN AN SIGNALED HIS MEN to move down the trail.

They had not moved more than about fifty yards when one of the men pointed to some disturbed earth on the side of the trail. The troops stopped, and An signaled them to check for mines and booby traps. They did, but they found none. One pulled a shovel from his pack and slowly dug some of the dry dirt on top of the hole. He had not been at it long when he announced with a smile of success that he had found something.

It was a cache of rifles. The men removed about a dozen Chicoms and a few MASs. They left the ammunition where it was, and when all the men had passed the site, they blew it. It was worthless to our troops because we all used carbines and a few M16s. If they had found AK-47s, it would have been different. It would have confirmed the apparent upgrading of the war. But, more importantly, we could have used them. They were better rifles than the M16.

An uneventful hour on the trail passed. It had already been a long morning. We halted, and the lunch preparations began.

Lunch was a ritual for these men. It wasn't the hastily consumed C-rations of the US troops. Captain An had a cook who prepared steamed rice and mixed in chopped fish. There were the long sticks of French bread from the bakery. Plenty of hot tea. And a sense of comfort. I felt like I was doing things right. We sat on the ground while the lunch preparations went on. An and I discussed what we had seen and what it meant. I felt like an advisor. It was not my knowledge that he sought. It was the opportunity for him to think out loud with someone he could trust.

There was a quiet period after lunch. The meal and my meandering thoughts of home, of Sunday meals, of another world, had a soporific effect. There was an absence of any command from headquarters to move out. They were also on lunch break. It was cool, at least in relative terms, sitting under a tree, a canal on one side and an open rice paddy on the other. It was, for the moment, idyllic. The men sat and smoked their strong cigarettes, chatting quietly. Captain An smoked, too, resting against a tree as he talked now with one of his lieutenants.

I was soon in a light catnap, the first time I had ever really relaxed on an operation. Time, during a catnap, can be an odd thing. You know you are there and present, yet somewhere else in a state of relaxation, floating back and forth. Suddenly I was awakened as one of the troops tapped my shoulder with a whisper of "Te We, *laida*" and a gesture to follow him away from the canal. I was mad at being caught off guard.

I followed, still awakening.

There was a sudden movement that finished the awakening process. A soldier pulled a grenade from his shoulder harness and lobbed in into the canal. The explosion was more of a thud than a bang as the small bomb went off in the water.

My eyes were everywhere at once. I had assumed that it had to be some VC trying to sneak back to the weapons cache.

But the troops were anything but wary. Five or so stripped to the waist and charged over the canal bank and down into the water. Suddenly, fish started appearing. The troops were picking them up from the surface and tossing them to the waiting cook on the bank. He cheerfully retrieved each one, putting it in a plastic sack.

I hadn't seen this kind of action before, but it made sense. The fish were barely hand size but essential protein to these troops, who were daily stressed by operations and provided minimal living support. And then it was sort of comic, full of humor, buffoonery, and laughter, a diversion from the tension of our work. My spirit was with them, these men with whom I fought.

We were soon back on the roadway walking toward Gò Công District. The old road markers in kilometers looked like something from the French countryside. Very simple, very utilitarian, no ornamentation. Just "14K" chiseled into the stone.

An hour or so later, we married up with Lieutenant Colonel Turnage. He was standing by a jeep surrounded by Vietnamese regular forces, looking over a map with his counterpart, Colonel Thieu.

Turnage liked to be in command and disliked being in the support position. Lieutenant Dane, who worked for Turnage, was near the jeep, observing the discussion. I joined the circle assembled around the hood of the jeep, a bit behind Captain An. An joined the circle while his men and the Vietnamese regular forces exchanged smiles, cigarettes, and quite talk. The captured rifles and AK-47 shells were examined and placed with the rest of the gear.

Turnage and his counterpart were not having a pleasant conversation. The talk was veiled with a false courtesy.

"Tell the colonel his troops must move faster. We must catch VC with AK-47s." The interpreter complied with Turnage's order.

Colonel Thieu's voice raised a pitch. The interpreter relayed Thieu's message but not his mood. "Colonel says his troops not move any faster. The US gunships should be making the contact with VC, Colonel says."

Turnage replied, "Gunships cost money to fly. When Vietnamese make contact, the gunships will come in. Not before."

I knew what was happening. I had seen this sort of exchange before, though without such hostility. Frankly, I would have done the same thing the Vietnamese colonel was doing had I been in his place. He did not want to make the first contact. His troops would invariably be killed. He would rather have the rich American army make that first contact and let the United States take the casualties if there had to be any, and the Vietnamese could mop up.

It was a common attitude among senior Vietnamese officers. Why should they finish the war? If they won, the US Army would leave, and that would leave them without money, equipment, attention. For senior officers at the center of things in war, national military victory would be a national economic disaster.

And Turnage was humiliating his counterpart in front of his men. It was a vanity trip for him. He knew he could not win. Turnage tried to sell the idea that was so contrary to the Vietnamese colonel's interest. It would only make the Vietnamese less likely to fight.

The command discussion came to an end. A small convoy formed. Turnage and Thieu in their jeeps and a truck full of bodyguards headed down the road.

Lieutenant Dane looked at Litzenger and me. "Glad that's over. They get to yelling at each other sometimes. Turnage even offered a bounty for any VC Thieu's men brought in."

I was caught off guard. I looked at him to see if he was smiling, as if he had joked. He wasn't.

"Seen any more Charlie?" he asked.

"None since the chopper took Weiner out."

"You know," Dane observed, "Weiner was a quarterback for his college team. He saw more combat every Saturday afternoon than most of us see in our tour. How bad was he?"

Litzenger caught my eye as he responded, "Just a surface wound." The combat shock was not mentioned. I understood.

"Well, good luck," Dane offered, putting on his rifle sling and joining his troops.

Captain An's company assembled and moved back into the trees. I moved into position about a third of the way in the line with An. My mind was moving into gear.

We stayed on the paths again, avoiding the open paddies. It grew hotter, more humid, and more debilitating with every step. I realized it was late in the afternoon, though without my watch, it didn't seem to matter to me what time it was. On an operation, I tended to measure time differently—not in terms of minutes, but in terms of degree of fatigue. Like an animal, I was constantly concerned with precious energy and when it could be replenished.

On the trail, I followed in the footprints of the Vietnamese soldier in front of me. I couldn't imitate the shuffling walk of the Vietnamese, but I knew the more Vietnamese I looked, the better my odds of survival.

Still, the explosion was unexpected.

At almost the same moment I heard it, I felt it, the pressure on my back. I thought I had been hit by a mine and just wasn't feeling the pain yet.

I turned, in that same second it seemed, with the sound in my ears. The Vietnamese soldier behind me had been blown apart. His torso was intact, but the small mine seemed to have gone right up him. What was on my back was part of him.

I had stepped right over the mine, leaving it for him. He was gone without so much as a human protest. Just gone. And there was no time then for the inevitable speculation about why.

As the blood and cloth were quickly buried and the remains were placed in a body bag, I walked down to the canal. Another Vietnamese soldier splashed water on my back to wash off the remains of what was once a man. The splashing seemed to go on forever, the time measured in stages of my emotions—shock, horror, fear, relief—and not in number of minutes.

"You look all right, Lieutenant," Litzenger offered. "How do you feel?"

I knew he was worried about another officer in shock.

"I'm OK, Sarge." Then I paused before I spoke my feelings. "Did you know him?"

"No, I didn't," he replied.

I looked at the Vietnamese quietly watching me as I walked up the bank. We moved on.

The sun was over the tree line when we stopped. The troops had carried the body bag, and its presence seemed to make the afternoon very still. There was little talk, just the occasional command.

I never did dry out in Vietnam. But this time my uniform was beginning to stink. I couldn't wait to get back and trash it.

"Ready for the helicopters," Captain An said.

I didn't hesitate. I knew it was time to pull out. I took the handset from the radio pack.

"Delta party, this is Big Boy," I began, "ready when you are. Over."

"Roger, Big Boy. Out."

So the wait began. We never knew when the choppers would arrive and couldn't ask over the radio. That kind of impatience would provide the listening VC with more than one ambush plan.

The artillery spotter plan circled overhead briefly to tell us that he was there.

"Big Boy, this is Bird Dog. I've got your location. Rest easy. Over."

"Roger, Bird Dog. Out."

Now we knew that if we drew fire, we could call in the big guns.

Captain An had his men fanned out to cover any direction of fire. We were still exposed. Our Bird Dog overhead had been monitoring our location, and it could take ten minutes or it could take an hour or more, depending on other troops they might have to take out.

Captain An called his cook and reached into the man's backpack. Pulling out a bottle of Old Forester, he turned to me. I was surprised but not unwilling. I reached into my own pack and extracted an empty C-ration can I had left from the last operation. An poured the warm brown liquid, and we drank slowly. It stung the roof of my mouth and then burned my chest as it went down. My sunburned body absorbed it with lust.

It was a celebration of sorts, at least for me. I had done my job, provided what was needed, and stayed out of the way, but I had learned from the professionals that some will try anything to get another to fight, even a bounty.

I pulled a box of Marlboros out of my pack and offered one to An. He smiled. I had learned to smoke on the first operation. It was less a pleasure than a necessity. I was burning the leeches off my legs as they wiggled up my boots and over the tape. Some of them managed to attach themselves right through the fabric of my trousers.

I remembered the C-ration of cake in my pack. I decided to pull it out and offer it to An. It was a grander gesture than it seemed.

The cake was a little piece of memory to me. The can top said, "One unit, cake, sugar, Interstate Brands Corporation, Kansas City, MO." It was more than a bit of home to me. With some difficulty, I pried the top off with the opener on my dog tag chain.

I offered it to An, who took a piece and handed the can back to me. The liquor and the cake were lightening the mood.

"Let the cook have the cake; I'll take the liquor," I jested.

"Moi aussi!" An laughed.

Soon, we heard the welcome whap-whap-whap-whap-whap of the choppers. Gunships swept along the tree lines, sporadically firing, covering the troop-carrying choppers as we boarded. And we were off, up into the cool air of a cloud-laden sky.

Home, I thought. Home, such as it is, to Sa Dec. Not home safe, but home alive.

Dear Mom and Dad,

A million thanks for the Care package. I got it in fine shape and started in with some Dermasol on my sunburn.

I got the burn today on an operation. Now what I mean by an operation is a little different from what you all must think. I usually stay at the command post with the Vietnamese general and the American colonel, of course, among their entourage. We listen to the radio to the different units of the division as they carry out their mission. I am the guy who observes when prisoners are interrogated. I do some other things, but all in all, it is mainly observing from our position in the operation.

Today, we had a few minutes of spare time, so my friend who is in charge of the interrogation and his two assistants joined me out in the paddies to practice with our rifles. We rode along the secure road, and I tried to speak Vietnamese with the people nearby, "observers of the event."

One of the things that I have worked hard on is the task of convincing the VN that they will get nothing out of the prisoners and suspects if they beat them. They have done this, and although it is not what I would call slapping them around, it is unnecessary. It was a personal task of mine, nothing that I have been taught in the army schools. We have had no cooperation from the prisoners, but I felt that it was wrong to manhandle them from the start. But we are advisors, and the first thing that we are taught is that we are to make suggestions, not demands. That is a tough task. The Vietnamese seem to go along with me.

Right now, I am munching on some of those Cracker Jacks. Hey, I have an idea for a candy. It is caramel-covered nuts. The Spanish peanuts in the Cracker Jacks are great, yet I have never seen them for sale alone. Mom, how about working out the recipe, and we'll be partners with the old man; what say?

Several questions: First, did you get the first money orders? I have enclosed $400 more in this letter. Let me know. Also, did you get the box with the robe? It is handmade here and costs about $8. It was the best she had.

By the way, I got Lippen off field duty. We had two new lieutenants coming in, and I pushed hard for one to take John's job. Now John will work at the HQ, and the other fellow, who wants to go to the field, will go in. I hope John will be and his wife and sister, too. Both have written me.

That's all the news for now. Take excellent care of each other and say hello to the Umbergers for me on your vacation. Dahlgren has sent a card, and I have sent a letter to her.

Love,
Paul

CHAPTER 5

❦

I STOOD AT THE COMPOUND bar one afternoon with my interrogation counterparts, Lieutenant Wa and Private Le.

We talked, as usual, about simple things. Not that Wa and Le weren't bright. Not that they weren't curious, too. There just was little possibility for intellectual discussion given the constraints of the sort of pidgin language we all used. Some English, some French, some Vietnamese. Our sentences were short; the thoughts, small and always about the present. Eye contact let us know if our comments were comprehended.

When we wanted to say more, Le would help out. But most often, Le sat, slightly away from us, quietly enjoying the security of the American club and the moments of calm in all of the distress around us. So, today, Le stood at the bar with us, listening and watching.

Le had continued to paint, and I had continued to encourage him. As I saw more of his work, I realized that he painted the same scene over and over and over again, each time more abstractly than before. The scene was a traditional Vietnamese landscape, a canal or river visible, a sampan waiting at its bank, and a thatched house on a rise behind. It was an expectant scene, as though at any moment, someone would emerge from the house, descend to the sampan, and be gone. In the first paintings, Le was mostly detailing the landscape, without people, peacefully at rest. But each rendering of a more recent scene grew more and more disturbing, more tortured, changing from simple depiction of reality to an alarming comment. In one, the yawning open space of the sampan was elongated like a scream, the thatch of the house almost orange, like hair on fire. In another, the scene was done in blue hues, as though through smoke. In another, the perspective was angled, as though seen from a banking helicopter. Le painted on anything he could find, including tent canvas; and in one, painted on burlap, the whole scene seemed to be melting away. It was a very personal thing between us: I, the observer and he, the commentator. I did not share his talent or my interest in it with anyone else.

On the other hand, my conversations with Lieutenant Wa more often left me with the feeling that he was directing things. He was curious and manipulative. He always seemed to be working to get me to talk about myself. He had a couple of techniques. The simplest was the endless stream of "Te We like?" questions.

The other was the unfailing reciprocal question. If I asked about his family, he asked about mine. Perhaps it was just a gracious act of an ancient culture expressed in the halting phrases of our pidgin speech, but I had speculated about it. And over the course of these conversations, we did get to know each other's backgrounds, interests, and desires.

Today, Wa was interested in my English classes. I had volunteered to teach English to local school children in the evenings. Le usually drove with me to the school.

"It's good you teach them. They must know English to be success, Te We," Wa observed. "Before, we speak French. If Vietnamese speak French, they get good jobs, good pay, live good life. Now, English same thing. You like to teach, Te We? You teach when you go home?" he asked.

I had not given much thought to my future. I knew a few things, though. I knew that my BA and a quarter would get me a cup of coffee. And I knew I was not meant for the army. I was at the top of my ROTC class because I knew my survival might depend on it. I had been offered a regular army commission but turned it down. Then, after college, I worked as a newspaper reporter, not as a career, more for the experience. Teaching seemed as good as anything at the moment.

"Yes, I like to teach. I like kids. You know, Wa, I can't understand it. In Vietnam, war is everywhere. Yet the Vietnamese kids I teach seem to smile all the time."

We laughed, and he gave me the same sort of smile I had seen on the faces of those young children who had so little to smile about. He offered no explanation. But his laugh told me he understood.

I waited, then added, "In USA, if I teach, I won't get good pay. I won't live good life."

Wa laughed again. "Same in Vietnam!" he agreed.

"And you? You want to teach?" I asked.

Wa's response was immediate.

"No, Te We, no. I stay in army. Once I want to be doctor, but now I stay in army." Wa looked thoughtful for a moment, then added brightly, "Wa maybe drive taxi in Saigon. Then Wa make much money! In Vietnam, officer and taxi driver get good pay, live good life."

"Yes, Wa. Good pay is important," I agreed. "Good pay important for your family."

"Wa not have family," he corrected.

"No family? Why?"

"No money, Te We!" he responded, and both he and Le laughed.

"I never get married, Te We," Le announced.

"Never, Le? Why not?"

"Because, Te We, Le never have money," Lee explained, still laughing.

I knew what he meant. He was too placid and too much an artist.

"Coe Faw nice person, Te We. Te We like?" Lieutenant Wa was at it again. Wa used the traditional term, *Coe*, for a young, single woman. Faw was the teacher whose students I taught English.

"Coe Faw is very smart. She is a good teacher," I responded with some caution. "She wants students to learn English."

With that, the round of beers ran out and so did our conversation. Wa left with Le, who dutifully reminded me that he would be back after supper to drive me to Sa Dec and Coe Faw's class.

When Le returned that evening, the jeep was driven by a soldier who insisted that he stay with the jeep. I understood the security and didn't mind the extra company. I hopped in, taking the front seat.

The drive was slow through the streets of Sa Dec. Families were gathering at home having dinner, fathers in boxer-like shorts standing in doorways, chatting with neighbors. It was a deceptive scene. It looked like it could be any neighborhood anywhere I had been, settling into early evening. Occasionally, the community television would dominate a street market with a commentator talking at the few assembled viewers. We passed the Shell Oil filling station, where several large freight trucks were waiting patiently for their fuel. They were in no rush. Once filled, they would wait overnight in town before moving their cargo into the country.

Dusk was a pleasant time in this war, the time when everyone seemed to feel a welcome lull between the high levels of activity of the day and the uncertainty of the night.

The school was alive with children chattering, playing, and then respectfully stopping to acknowledge me as Le and I passed them. It was difficult for me to tell their ages. Most seemed to be in their teens. They dressed alike in uniforms like kids in private schools back home; the boys wore white shirts and trousers of dark shades; the girls wore the traditional *ao dai* dress with a split tunic over black pants.

Occasionally, one would be bold enough to offer up what I had taught them was a proper greeting. "Hello, Te We, how are you tonight?" Usually this would be a young man, not the bashful girls. Then he and the others would giggle as I stopped to respond and encourage.

Coe Faw was waiting at her desk. Lieutenant Wa's question lingered uncomfortably on my mind as I entered. I did indeed like Coe Faw. In fact, she grew more attractive to me every time I saw her. Her face was lovely and round; her hair, long and black, pulled back at the nape of her neck and hanging straight to her waist.

"Welcome, Te We. You are very kind to come." She stood and greeted me. Le faded off to the side.

"I'm glad to help."

I was. I told myself that I was making at least some contribution to the minds of Vietnam's children.

Faw called the class to attention. I opened my book as I did each evening here. This experience was a total contradiction to my time out on operations or on convoy duty or staying up all night in the operations center.

We used a simple method of instruction. Faw would say a word or a sentence, and the class would repeat it in unison. It was traditional rote learning, but it was proven effective. I corrected pronunciation or occasionally amused the class by acting out a word or idea.

After many classes, the students give me a special gift

The word "blow" was giving them a hard time that evening. I closed my lips and then gently blew my lips out, saying the word and showing the meaning at the same time with a bit of humor to implant it in their minds. The class loved it. Faw blushed slightly.

The class ended, as it always did, with a chorus of "Thank you!" from the standing students. Le returned to the classroom with another teacher and introduced her. Coe Moi smiled at me, and as she did so, I had a fleeting moment of reminder. Her smile was familiar, rather like that of one of my boyhood crushes.

Coe Moi was every bit as attractive as Faw, though she was dressed with a little more attention to style and ornament. Like Faw, she wore traditional garb, but her blouse was embroidered. Unlike Faw, her English was minimal. She taught much younger children who were not yet studying the language.

"Te We help Faw," Coe Moi began, smiling and trying to communicate. "Faw my…" She stopped to consult Le. "Roommate!" she finished triumphantly. "Te We like Vietnam?"

The proverbial introductory question. But I did want to encourage her.

"Yes. Te We likes Vietnam. Te We likes helping Faw. Te We likes Le, too. Le is a fine man and teaches me."

Le laughed at that. Blushing at the praise, he rather shyly explained it to Moi. She blushed, too, as if to support his embarrassment.

Moi consulted Le again, a longer inquiry this time.

Le translated, "Moi wants to know about your home, your family."

I was certainly not unwilling to answer, but I had to be back at the compound before curfew.

"Maybe Faw and Moi have lunch with me tomorrow," I suggested. It would be Saturday, when I assumed they didn't teach, and I had no duty.

A brief consultation with Le, and it was arranged.

We met in town at a restaurant open to the street with no doors, a tile floor, and several simple wooden tables set for four. I was initially uncomfortable with this kind of exposure, my security sense asserting itself. I sat with my face toward the street, but a grenade would be fatal for all of us.

Wa did the ordering for us. Iced tea appeared with a bowl of the large brown sugar crystals, then rice, vegetables, and meat. My three guests took a set of chopsticks from the glass at the center of the table, and each in ritualistic fashion wiped them carefully with their white paper napkins before eating.

I learned little during the first of the lunches. Conversation was complicated. Moi would ask. Le would help. I would answer. Le would explain, and then there would be some conversation between the two women. And all the time Wa would listen. It was hard to cover much ground. But it was pleasant, and we always agreed to meet again.

I liked these lunches. They were a respite from the routine of the war. Despite their youthful appearances, Faw and Moi were, I learned, just a few years younger than Wa and me. I grew to appreciate the gentle elegance of both of them. They walked with the slow grace of their class, quite unlike the sliding gait of peasant women. They dressed not in black pants and blouses but always in the *ao dai* dresses that were seductively slit to the waist, allowing a momentary view of curving hip line when they moved. Of the two, Faw was the more serious, the more mature. She asked fewer questions, seemed to be quieter and more analytic. Moi was full of uninhibited energy in conversation, wanting to know about everything, always asking questions, and always smiling at the answers. I found myself chatting easily in this company, and it felt good. We talked about everything including politics, there and at home.

It was a year before election time, and Nixon already appeared to be winning, but I had been surprised to hear about what was called "unrest about the war" over the radio. No one had written to me about this. *Everyone was being careful*, I thought. Letters to me were not about the problems of life and politics but rather were focused on the simple reference points to sanity and security: my family, my sister's new son, weather at home, Dad's business.

I did the same thing. When I talked with my Vietnamese friends, it was not about the daily realities of military duty, but about the people, the weather, the "real life." We talked about our homes and about family events, of brothers and sisters. Once, we toasted with our glasses of tea the birth of my brother's first child.

Just as I was assuming that the lunches were a permanent part of my life, they came to an end. It was, of course, Lieutenant Wa who was all knowing.

"Coe Moi go to Saigon soon," he announced one evening at the compound's bar, pausing from his attention to the condensation on the outside of a cold, American beer can.

"Coe Moi?" I was astonished. "Why?"

"Not know, Te We."

"She did not tell us about this. Why would she do that? She will lose job here," I persisted.

"Te We, I do not have answer." Wa looked thoughtful for a moment and added, "Te We, you have lunch with me tomorrow."

Another surprise and impossible to reject. It was the first time I felt Wa was opening up his personal life to me. We had been working together for some months now, sharing hours of comparing notes from interrogations, looking for facts and correlations in reports from the field. Since our first encounter, Wa had never used torture in interrogations, at least in my presence, and he had apparently spread the word. I had heard that one Vietnamese unit, notorious for dragging prisoners behind their armored personnel carriers, had stopped this practice when Wa informed the commander that surely the Te We would report this and there would be dire consequences and loss of face.

But Wa had never shown a willingness to invite me into his personal life.

It was a pleasant lunch at a Sa Dec restaurant with Wa and two of his fellow Vietnamese officers. We ate the same food that one always ate in Vietnam: rice, chopped meats and spices, iced tea, Ba Mui Ba beer (a national beer with "33" on the label). The waiter was gracious, either to keep in favor with the army or to get us to return or both. As we said our goodbyes outside the restaurant, Wa began walking with me toward his jeep.

"Coe Moi like to see you now, Te We."

I looked at him in surprise. "This afternoon?"

"OK?" he asked.

"Yes, fine. OK." At least I would have the chance to talk to her about going to Saigon.

Wa ushered me to his jeep and drove to the center of town. A block from the canal that separated the two from the compound, I saw Moi walking down the steps of a building with apartments over the first-floor shop. She exchanged pleasantries with Wa as I got out of the jeep, and then Wa drove off.

Moi was smiling, as always. She led me up the steps and to the door of her apartment. She opened the door and gestured for me to enter.

"Coe Faw in Can Tho. You like tea?"

We drank.

Suddenly shy, she looked at the floor. "I go to Saigon soon."

"Yes, I know. Wa told me. But why?" I tried to hold her gaze, looking for an answer.

She smiled again, ignoring my question. Then, quietly, she said, "Moi like Te We." She grabbed my hand and held it tightly. "Moi think Te We very handsome. Te We like Moi?"

I tried to control my interest. Forgetting my own question, I said, "Te We thinks Coe Moi is very pretty."

Sophisticated language was hardly needed.

"Moi make love with Te We." Her comment was everything—a question, a statement, and most of all an exclamation.

She kept my hand in hers, leading me to a second room with two wooden twin-size beds. The beds had three-inch pads of hard thatch or straw and were covered with white sheets. The room was dim, lit only by the indirect rays of the afternoon sun coming through the windows of the main room. White mosquito nets were draped back to both sides of the beds.

I had no hesitation. She began carefully unbuttoning the blouse of her *ao dai* and I watched her, captivated. Then I began.

She was small and delicate in bed but warm and as energetic as her questions and conversations. She giggled and pointed as she discovered the hair on my chest. Her body was completely smooth, the color of almonds. It clashed for a moment with the white of mine, then seemed to harmonize.

I began to kiss her softly on the lips. She moved her head instinctively to one side and then gently sniffed at my cheek.

"We not kiss in Vietnam," she explained. "Maybe you teach me."

"I teach."

I walked down the steps of the apartment building without Moi. She said goodbye dressed in a robe.

I looked around. Wa was nowhere to be seen. But I was seen. A Vietnamese soldier sitting across the street, stopped sipping tea and yelled. Wa appeared, running up the street from a restaurant.

"You and Coe Moi have good time?" he asked as we walked toward his jeep.

Embarrassed, I said, "Coe Moi is a very nice person." It seemed impossible that Wa didn't know, but I felt some deference to our privacy.

"Te We, you know Moi go to Saigon very soon," he said as he started the engine. "Her father find job for her at friend's restaurant. Moi make money and have good life. Not like teacher."

Again, Wa was feeding me small portions of what he knew. There was my answer. Wa was describing, as gently as he could, the life of a Saigon bar girl. I knew it. As mellowed as I was by our time together, as melted with the emotion of release, I hated it.

Wa said nothing else on the way back to the compound. I was alone with my slowly recovering senses and my confusion.

I returned to the duties of the field and the briefing room, but I thought constantly of Moi for days, though it was almost impossible to see her. "Very soon" meant weeks to the Vietnamese.

Moi did not leave very soon for Saigon. She stayed in Sa Dec for over a month, and we saw each other twice more over a weekend when Faw had gone. Moi and I were together: she, the cheerful, submissive partner, and I, the lover trying to get her to stay as much for myself as out of concern for her future work as a hooker.

On the last of these occasions, Moi had reached from the bed to a table beside it and handed me a sky-blue scarf made of a fine wool, intricately woven and tied.

"I give to you to remember Moi."

Moi was full of plans. She teased me when I suggested that she continue teaching.

"Maybe Te We and Moi live together in Sa Dec," she proposed.

The trap that I was falling into was of my own creation. The Moi who was not in it with me was different. And so was I.

After Moi left, I continued to teach classes. Faw was polite but distant.

There were to be no more of the pleasant lunches with Le and Wa.

I realized that this war was making prostitutes of Vietnam's teachers and taxi drivers of its doctors.

Dear Brenda and the Gang,

Many thanks for the two great letters. All these glowing reports about Andy make me feel thankful that he has such a fine family to watch after him.

My fair skin and I are, shall I say, faring well. As you can well imagine, the sun is a little more direct here so that just a few minutes in the sun can really get to you. The few times that I have gotten too much sun, Dad's Dermosol did the trick. That is the best that I have used.

My job here is getting more and more runaround. But it's a funny type of runaround. Last week, I was gone every day on operations. This week, I think right now I'll be around all the time. I have recently gotten the Special Services job thrust upon me, so that is another task, but I shall try to enjoy that, too. It is the one task that I have that I, alone, can see what progress I am making. We are planning a tennis match between two men, the advisor and his counterpart. General *** loves the game, and the colonel plays, also. We'll put them together, though, not separated. Then, a volleyball game between the VN and the US teams. This is besides the normal stuff and a bingo game. Got any suggestions? Having served as an officer's wife, an old pro like you should know lots of such things. What do you think?

This work schedule also might explain the reason for the sporadic letters. But I try to keep Mom and Dad informed twice a week.

Could you do me a favor? I need about five sets of intelligence brass and about five infantry cross rifles. Can

Bill get them at Fort Knox? They are perfect to give to the VNs for doing favors. How about sending 'em some?

Another thing I might ask of you: I would like to have some tapes, especially jazz. Could you make me some? Have you heard Sergio Mendez and Brasilia 66? They are favorites of mine. Let me know what the tapes costs, and I shall send you a check.

I'm also glad to hear that Bill is doing so well. I was wondering about his success as a career officer if he returns to college. I couldn't be a career officer. Presently, I plan to return to get a master's. The other day, a strange phenomenon overcame me. I realized that I was twenty-three and really didn't believe it. I really haven't evaluated its significance yet either. Tomorrow, we head out on an operation, so I think that since we have a lot of time just waiting, I'll think about it. Is this a phase?

I better close. Keep excellent care of the family! I find that when I care for something intensely, I look after myself a little better. That, of course, is a subtle hint to take care of yourself, each of you.

Love,
Your brother,
Paul

CHAPTER 6

⚜

CHRISTMAS, 1967, WAS HARDLY A time of joyful celebration for us advisors at Sa Dec. No matter what we did—plastic Christmas trees with ornaments, gift drawing, lots of booze, we all knew we were missing our families. And Moi was gone.

There was the promise of peace for the holiday period. Tet, the Vietnamese New Years, fell within weeks of our New Year. The VC offered a truce to give us a break. In return, Vietnamese and US forces had halted search-and-destroy operations.

As I sat in the operations center on Christmas Eve, listening to nothing on the radio from the provinces. There was no indication of what was about to happen.

The mess hall was decorated. The cook had tried to put together something special. There was turkey, mashed potatoes, cranberry sauce, rolls and butter. The pièce de résistance was a Christmas cake. The cook had made it out of an excess of cake mixes used for birthdays. He wanted to get rid of them. We joked about it. But Christmas is a birthday.

Christmas week passes slowly, an ironic twist. No war meant boredom and home sickness.

Shortly after New Year's Day, I got the word that I would be taking the convoy to Saigon for supplies. It would take us three days if all went well. I had done it twice before and learned that being a convoy officer was a sinecure. The real man in charge was Sergeant Yankolovich, who was a pro. There were always more volunteer NCOs than needed to do the driving. The assignment, though, meant an evening or two in Saigon for them, which sounded good to all of us. I had several friends with the 525 Military Intelligence Group whom I could see. And I might locate Moi. Fat chance.

Sergeant "Yank" assembled the convoy vehicles. It would start with ten or so vehicles and progressively grow as we picked up small convoys from the other units traveling the same route. On convoy, the most important vehicle of the bunch was the tow truck. It seemed that no matter how hard the maintenance guys tried, something always broke down on the road. They didn't like being sitting ducks repairing a vehicle on the road any better than the rest of us.

The general held a party for the advisors on Christmas day. He was Roman Catholic, one of the issues that divided the Vietnamese, since most in power were catholic and the rest were Buddhist. It was the first time that I, a low-ranking officer among the advisors, had been in the general's home, even though it was located just at the entrance to the advisors' compound. Afterward, I spent about an hour in the spirit of mutual celebration and then retired for an early call for the convoy departure in the morning.

"Lieutenant!"

I was hailed by Sergeant Wilson, the supply manager, running toward me from the headquarters building. "Lieutenant, I've got to talk to you. Whatever you bring back, make sure you bring some good booze. The colonel likes his scotch." He paused for a moment, wiping his brow, then continued, "Lieutenant, I'm serious. The last load of booze was terrible. If you don't deliver with this load, I'll get skinned alive, and I'll have to tell the guy that you were in charge." His joke put me on the spot.

I understood. The last convoy had brought back three pallets of Royal Crown Cola, green crème de menthe, and Pabst Blue Ribbon beer.

For thirty days, the club had been the site of some major demonstrations in the chemistry as we tried every combination of the three, tried some of them on fire, tried them warm, iced, mixed with food colors. It was that or see the same movie for three nights in a row. And it was, after all, Christmastime, when we all remembered things back home.

I was still learning the ins and outs of resupply in Saigon, but I promised to do my best. I had learned a fair amount, however, about the necessary currency.

In my months at Sa Dec, I had acquired a small arsenal. My locker contained, in addition to my M16, a twelve-gauge shotgun, my derringer, a 9 mm pistol, and at least a dozen VC rifles that included Chicoms, German World War II Mausers, French MAS, and a French Etienne.

The rifles were the currency for resupply. Once, when we needed a special trip on one of the Chinook helicopters for a load of recreation supplies from Vung Tau, I suddenly became the man to see. I was amazed at the values in trade. For two VC rifles to be used as war souvenirs, I got a US Army captain to fly in a load that included ping pong balls, a ping pong table, volley balls, tennis equipment, and even a set of water skis. The water skis had yet to be used. The navy had offered its patrol boats to tow anyone, but no one had the guts to try. There was a jar filled with military chit awaiting anyone who changed their minds and would water ski on the river in full view of VC snipers.

I checked the contents of my locker that night, trying to figure out what would bring in bar supplies. I paused as I closed the locker door. I had taped up a picture of my parents, Libba, one of myself with Faw's students, and a small black-and-white picture of Moi. I planted a quick kiss on my hand, transferring it to the door.

I counted my chit to make sure I had enough for Saigon. It was fifteen dollars a night at the hotel where we would stay. Then there would be meals, a stop at the USO, which was the only place I knew I could get something close to the kind of slushy ice cream I had loved since I was a kid. If I found Moi, I needed enough for dinner with her. I knew, even as I planned the evening and the finances in my head, that it was unlikely I would find Moi. It was Tet, and she could very well be with her family at Chau Duc on the Cambodian border.

I crawled under the mosquito netting that was held a few feet above the four corners of my bunk, tied to wooden upright sticks. I had a few moments of the kind of hollowness that sets in during the holidays and when nothing important to me was near. The trip really boiled down to surviving two long days of travel and two days of doing little in Saigon. Sleep came quickly.

But it was short.

"Mortars incoming! Mortars!"

By the sound of the impact of the second mortar, all eight of us officers in my hooch were charging as fast as we could to the bunker. I was closest to the door. I instinctively grabbed my rifle and steel pot.

Outside, I dropped down on all fours to scramble into the bunker and heard the screams from inside the bunker.

"Jesus! Grenades everywhere! Stay out! Holy shit!"

Mortar rounds landed, and in the panic of the moment, with all of us scrambling, pushing, I moved into the bunker at a crawl. The danger outside was real. The danger inside the bunker was perceived. We had no choice.

I could not believe my hands and what they encountered in the dark. There were grenades all over the floor of the bunker.

"If there's one with a loose pin, we're scrambled eggs!" someone said. "Be careful."

The instinct to survive overcame the panic and seemed to capture every muscle in each of the men. In the dark, everyone gently laid their rifles down and began feeling around on the floor, picking up the grenades, checking with the light touch of their fingers to see if the pins were still securely in place. Then, quietly, we passed the grenades through the dark to the man closest to the grenade box.

Outside, behind us, around us, there were the sounds of the mortars.

"Charlie is putting on one hell of a New Year's celebration for us," said one voice, awed.

When the mortars stopped, gunfire could be heard from about a half mile away near the town's edge. Then more gunfire. And more. It seemed to be coming from all three directions surrounding the compound. The mortar fire subsided. It was not for our benefit. It meant that Charlie would now attack.

Two men mounted the top of the bunker with the M60 machine gun. I sat inside at the front, where there was a horizontal slot about a foot long that looked out onto the compound's entrance. Behind me at the back of the bunker, men were sitting, tense, sweating in the dark, unsure of what was happening.

Peering out, my ears were more useful than my eyes. "The gunfire is getting closer," I said. "How many of you guys have sixteens?"

Four did.

"Maybe we should go back to the hooch and get them," said a voice tentatively.

"Get them." The voice was clearly identifiable in the dark. It was a senior captain.

The men were out and back in what seemed less than a minute, though walking fifteen feet to the hooch was an eternity of exposure if a mortar round came in. The mortars had stopped, though, because the attack had begun.

The darkness was now filled with sounds of rifle fire, counter fire, commands in two languages, yells of anxiety, occasional machine gun bursts, closer rifle fire, then more counter fire.

I could just make out some movement. The general's guards, apparently rather relaxed with the festivities, had made it back to their posts. By protecting the general's quarters, they were protecting us.

Slowly and surprisingly, the silence between weapons fire grew until there was quiet. The quiet came as eight men sweated in an eight-by-eight-by-three-foot-high space surrounded by dirt-filled plastic bags.

"Take your positions!" a voice commanded.

I couldn't decide for a moment which was worse: the dark bunker with its acrid smell of fear or the outside with its light humid breeze and the potential of being hit with a mortar shell or an errant bullet.

We spread out and knelt behind the fifty-five-gallon barrels that lined the fence and marked out the compound. Our two NCOs with the machine gun watched. It was Major LaRue who came by to check on us. There was the first faint light of the morning.

"Charlie is on the attack all over the country," he explained in a quiet monotone. "We got through with a few minor injuries. Everybody OK here?" he asked.

"Fine, sir," we answered in staccato fashion.

"Here's the situation," LaRue continued. His tone of command was designed to reassure us that we had everything under control, but he had other men to brief. "The general and his men were together celebrating when the attack came. Otherwise, we would have had no protection. He wouldn't have had any either."

There was just the hint of a low murmur among us as we collectively realized what that meant. We were next door to the general's quarters. Our bunker would have been hit first.

"Now, everyone stay low for another ten minutes," LaRue ordered. "If it stays quiet, get back to your hooches and get ready. They may come again. Half of you go, and half of you stay here until the others return."

We did, still watchful. But the battle was over, at least for Sa Dec.

By break of day, the officers were assembled in the briefing room with rifles and battle gear and bodies smelling of the fear and the uncertainty of war.

"As best we know, the VC made a full-scale attack all over the country. They are in Saigon, but they seem to be stopped and are fighting in pockets." Colonel Bough reviewed the situation, and we listened with an intensity I had not felt before.

"We still have some problems," Bough continued. "Vinh Long and Vinh Binh are overrun. Chau Duc is not reporting. It looks bad there. The VC took out most of our helicopters at Vinh Long airfield, and anything and anyone that can fly is doing medevac."

He moved his pointer across the map, and the reality sank in. Lip was in Vinh Long. Moi was probably in Chau Duc.

"The general has decided to send troops to Vinh Long to secure the airfield. Pritchard," Bough pointed, "you go with the ARVN convoy to take Captain An's men to Vinh Long. Keep radio con. Good luck."

That was that. The airfield was critical. It was two hours to Vinh Long, and it was open country all the way. We'd be lucky to make it.

I checked every round in my pack as I moved out. I watched as Vietnamese soldiers marched into the compound with prisoners taken in the night. Most VC walked without shoes and in black pajama uniforms. Some were bloody, and several looked about the right age for Faw's classroom, about twelve or thirteen years old. I stared. Some were wearing ARVN uniforms.

"How the hell did those grenades get out?" It was Sergeant Litzenger, joining me as An checked his men. The story must have spread fast.

"Who knows?" I hadn't had time to think about that. "Maybe one of the cleaning women sabotaged us."

Litzenger looked at me thoughtfully. He mounted the back of a deuce truck with a squad of Vietnamese.

"Up here, Lieutenant."

I looked up. Litzenger had his rifle, confirming what I already knew. This was serious. I was tempted to join him because he knew where the safest place would be. We would be up high. We could shoot in any direction or jump out of the open truck. But I was the captain's advisor, and I knew I had to be with An in the lead jeep.

I shook my head, and Litzenger shrugged. I walked toward An's jeep, my instinct telling me that, if An's jeep got hit, everyone would be hit. Normally, I sat on my flak jacket in case a bomb went off under our jeep. But this time I kept it on. Rifle fire was my first concern.

The convoy moved slowly through Sa Dec, taking side streets rather than the main road to the highway connecting us to Vinh Long. An had obviously thought this through carefully, as he did any maneuver. If there were going to be an ambush in the city streets, it would more likely be on the main road the convoys usually took and not on the side streets.

The houses were quiet. There was none of the usual coming and going of the morning. But I was surprised to see that there was very little damage in Sa Dec. The small market on the outskirts of the town had seen the only fire fight and now appeared to be controlled by ARVN troops. Wounded people and prisoners must have already been taken away. All that remained of the night's activity were a few buildings in rubble from direct hits of the mortar fire, the black char from explosions, and the burning of small fires caused by explosives and tracer rounds. The town's radio loudspeaker was blaring the news in Vietnamese, and I could almost understand it. In any language, the tone was clear: Everything is under control. We are in command. We are the victors. The other guys are the bad guys. See what they've done?

The convoy moved on, heading down the side of the river on the old road. Occasionally, we passed a small village, but still no one came out of their houses. In these smaller places, people were not inside listening to radios. They were still listening to the voices of their fears.

The first roadside fort of the ARVN Popular Forces that we encountered had been heavily hit. There were five men left. Two were wounded and being treated by the other three.

Captain An and I approached, and An spoke to them at some length; then, turning to me, he explained in French, "They were overrun. Hit quickly. The VC offered them their lives if they surrendered. Eight men went over, and the VC shot at the ones who stayed behind. Then the VC headed for Sa Dec."

It made sense to me. This little fort was peanuts last night. They were going for Sa Dec. Those who surrendered would be at the front of the VC assault line.

We helped the wounded onto a truck and left the other three Vietnamese with two of An's men. An wanted to secure the road and had brought several extra men along for this sort of circumstance. The men left behind watched us, nervously, as we started moving again.

I understood this fear, but they would be all right. It seemed to me from the morning briefing that Charlie had overextended himself. He planned to take the US compound and the Vietnamese general. But the Vietnamese soldiers were still together, celebrating Tet. The luck seemed to be running our way, and at that moment luck seemed more important in this war than forethought and experience. *Luck runs out though*, I thought, glancing back at the countryside, everywhere at once.

I took out my cigarettes and offered one to An. I did not smoke much. I might burn them to stop leeches. I couldn't remember ever having a cigarette so early in the day. But I smoked now and took comfort in it. After last night and now sitting in the back of a canvas-covered jeep, speeding off to

God-knew-what, it seemed appropriate. Precedent seemed irrelevant. It was the first moment in which I had breathed deeply for about twelve hours.

To our amazement, we reached Vinh Long without incident. But it made sense. The countryside and the villages were not important to Charlie. This was an offensive for the towns and cities. At the outskirts of the town, it was clear that Vinh Long had taken and was still taking a much heavier toll than Sa Dec.

Gun fire rang out. Captain An reacted instantly, halting the convoy and ordering his men out. They formed two lines along either side of the trucks and began walking toward a bridge that led into the center of the town. The walk was slow, the thought of death in every man's mind. An and I both knew from the briefing that there would be no US artillery or gunships to call on.

The first sounds were snipers' rifle shots. Captain An ordered his men to take cover and return the fire. It was intense but brief. It might have been the quick, accurate response from An's men, or it might have been an evacuation by the VC, but the fire stopped abruptly, and An ordered his men to mount up again.

As we moved forward toward the town and the airfield, I realized that An had no choice. It would have taken the rest of the day just to get to the center of Vinh Long if we walked and allowed each sniper to slow us down. At a reasonable speed, we were a big target, but we could get to the center of town within minutes.

There was no sniper fire as we approached the center of the town. Like most Vietnamese towns, Vinh Long's heart was where two crossroads met, with the market, the main government headquarters, and the government radio loudspeakers.

They'd had one hell of a fight at Vinh Long. People were starting to move around, cleaning up now, rebuilding sandbag protections at the entrance to the government building, picking up the wounded and bodies. Some of the wounded were still leaning against building walls.

The convoy stopped, and Litzenger joined me. We both ran to the advisor's quarters, where we found one flustered private in the compound, manning the radio.

"We got it pretty bad, but everyone is OK." He pointed off to his right. "They went down there. There's a hospital over that way. There's still fighting."

Litzenger and I left the private and returned to Captain An to relay the message. An didn't hesitate.

"We go to hospital."

Litzenger and I jumped in his jeep in agreement.

The convoy got a few blocks from the town square before taking fire. Then, almost immediately, we were picking up rifle fire all around us. The convoy needed no command to stop. We started on foot, slowly working our way along the building walls, cautiously and then in spurts, moving building to building. The shooting increased all the way to the hospital, and as we approached, I could see that part of the building was in flames.

"We got the fuckers on the run!"

My concentration broke for a moment.

It was not the English words. It was the Southern accent. It was Lip. He was running toward us from around the corner of the hospital.

"Hey!" I called out. "Lip! You OK?"

He heard me. He smiled, then disappeared around another corner. I started to follow him but stopped, my concentration broken completely and my concern for Lip. He was doing his job. I focused on mine.

Then there were screams.

From the entrance to the hospital a Vietnamese nun appeared, shouting and gesturing. No translation was needed. I glanced up at the building. The flames were engulfing it now.

I ran up to the entrance and into chaos. Nuns and anyone able were helping patients down the hallways and toward the door. People were wailing. Some were in shock. Bloody gauze seemed to cover the people helping the patients. Some of these were wounded soldiers. Many were just plain sick people.

But it was the baby. Not an adult, not a soldier. It was a baby, bloody and limp, being offered to me by a distraught Vietnamese nun. For a second, I didn't think my arms could hold this burden. I knew my heart could not. I thought the baby was dead as the nun pointed off toward the hospital door.

My M16 hung from the sling on my right lower arm, just behind the child's head.

I looked at her, then at the baby.

"Why?" My face must have said it in some eternal expression.

She pointed insistently, and the baby cried out.

"VC shoot!" she shouted at me, as though even the facts could not explain this insanity.

I was frozen with the baby draped over my arms.

"VC shoot! Understand? VC shoot! Papa American!"

I did understand.

I ran down the hall, cradling this child, following the nurses to get this symbolic child to safety.

There were other nuns moving among the evacuated patients, administering aid. One of them took the child.

Then I was in a daze of hatred.

When I found Captain An with his men, I was ready for anything. Ready for revenge, ready for a VC at close range, through the heart.

"Hey, Pritchard!" Litzenger called out. "We're moving in on the airfield. Fire fight seems to be over there."

I hadn't noticed.

"How are they doing at the hospital?" Litzenger asked.

"Fucking VC…" I said, with each syllable long and drawn out.

He seemed to understand.

"Come on, Lieutenant. Let's go."

We ran. We shot everywhere. We did what our training taught. But now training boiled in a cauldron with hate and unanswerable questions.

The airfield was a mess. Helicopters were burning all along the field. The pilots and crews were still in their bunkers. There were a few shots from the tree line, but it seemed that the VC had done the damage they were going to do and had melted into the countryside.

"They caught us with our pants down," said the US major as Captain An's men helped secure the field.

I stayed with An and got a status report off to Sa Dec that said about the same thing. It didn't seem to sum up the senselessness I felt. The colonel seemed calm on the other end of the radio.

"Roger. Stay put. Maintain control. Out."

But I was not in control. I wanted to return to the hospital, but Litzenger stopped me.

"Nothing to do there, Lieutenant. The fire's out. Everybody's OK."

I was suddenly and utterly exhausted. It was now late afternoon. It was closing in on a day that began in the dark and the stench of fear in the bunker. I had not eaten anything. I had been running on the calories of the last meal.

I felt Litzenger nudging me. We both walked a few feet away from the makeshift command center Captain An's men had established, and we sank to the ground. There, leaning against the right rear tire of a two-and-a-half-ton truck, we rested.

"Lieutenant...the colonel wants you," Litzenger gestured toward the radio.

I took the mike.

"Roger. This is Pritchard. Over."

"We've got a chopper coming in for you. They have your orders. Good job." The colonel's tone was clipped and restrained.

Within minutes, I could hear and then see the chopper. It was from the US Ninth Division. Litzenger and I walked toward the landing spot as it descended.

"Lieutenant Pritchard!" shouted the pilot over the roar.

"Right!" I shouted back, waving and running toward the waiting chopper. I pointed back behind me. Litzenger hadn't moved. "Litzenger also?"

"No, sir!" the pilot shook his head. "Our orders are to take you to the *USS Benowah*. Just you. General's orders, sir!"

Litzenger heard. He was already a short distance away, heading back to the command center, casually saluting me.

I jumped aboard, too tired to question.

In seconds, we were over the town, climbing as quickly as the pilot dared. Then we were over the river and heading downstream. I strained to see the town that began to look miniature as we rose. There was smoke rising from burning buildings. I made out the hospital. There were smoldering fires everywhere.

The air rushing into the open chopper grew cooler with every second. It was refreshing but I could not relax. What were these new orders, I wondered.

Craning my neck, I watched the outline of the hospital disappear. I sat back. The picture of the nun and the memory of the baby in my arms flooded my brain. The memory was worse, far worse than the moment itself. With the picture that wouldn't go away in my eyes, I wondered if I were actually capable of the same act. The VC who shot the baby was also a soldier.

I sank forward, closing my eyes.

The chopper was on the square pad atop a gray floating troop carrier. I jumped out onto the surface of the pad, surprised at the number of navy crews guiding the helicopters. All American.

A US Army lieutenant ran to me below the whirling blades.

"This way, Lieutenant."

I followed him to the gray door, then up a tight hall.

"Welcome to the US Ninth," he said as we walked. "I understand you're the guy who is going to guide us into more Charlie out of Vinh Long."

"I guess so," I replied. The next hours were spent with briefing the officers who would fly in with me to Vinh Long airfield, secure it, and then be ready to move to other targets. I worked in a shower and was shown the officers' mess, even got ice cream.

When our helicopter armada landed at Vinh Long, I introduced the officers to Captain An, in French. His men had not had the showers or clean uniforms that I had had on the *U.S.S. Benowah*, but they did seem to have gotten some rest and food.

Litzenger was down by the canal. The US troops had set up an artillery battalion of 105 howitzers on the bank. They were providing a sheet of fire in front of the Vietnamese troops, cleaning up the countryside. The sound itself was a concussive.

"Hey, Lieutenant!" Litzenger returned my greeting. "Check this." He swept his arm along the canal. "Charlie left mines everywhere. The ARVN think that our shelling will detonate them."

It was a joke, and we both knew it. Wasting expensive shells would do little to clear out the mines.

We stood, watching the volleys being fired, saying nothing, and then staring as a small sampan came into view. The howitzers were silent. The sampan moved up the canal, carrying a Vietnamese man and woman, who seemed unconcerned. Possibly they thought the shelling was over. And their life had to go on.

Then, in a pounding instant, a howitzer shell exploded right over the sampan, the force of it blowing them both out of the boat and into the waters of the canal. In that instant, the boat was gone. I was convinced that it was certain death for the man and woman. So few Vietnamese seemed to know how to swim. Then several US soldiers were in the water, miraculously pulling two struggling people toward the bank. Litzenger and I ran toward them.

"I can't believe it!" Litzenger said. "They're lucky to be alive!"

I was silent for a moment. "I don't know about that," I said.

Dear Mom and Dad,

No, I'm not seeing red, Mom and Dad. I just started to type with this thing on red and thought it wasn't a bad idea.

It's about nine thirty in the evening. I was just talking with my interpreter. He asked me for a special gift, and I got it today in Can Tho. It's a pair of boots. Isn't it strange how something so unimportant to one person can mean so much to another? he has asked me several times. Today, I was in Can Tho on business and picked up a pair for him. He just left, but before going, he said over and over and over, "Tank you vely much, sir." The guy has been an invaluable friend to me. He was the one who showed me around Sa Dec, who shared the experience with me at the pagoda. Anyway, he just walked out the door with boots-new boots-strung over his shoulder, a proud smile on his face, and the words of one filled with excitement but thinking about what he is saying, "See you later."

I was very happy to receive your two letters today. I must say that I, too, am a little concerned about the delay in mail delivery. Several have mentioned it to me about their letters home, too. For instance, your letter was postmarked on the fifteenth and got here on the nineteenth. That is great. Now, how long does it take my letters to get home?

Dad, your determination is like a lion before a long-awaited feast. But, please, please don't work yourself too hard. I agree with you that it is good to see the business from the books to the building. I, in no way, can suggest where you should relax or when. This you must do.

Remember that a man of your age is very lucky. He has lived to an age that maybe half of his peers will make. He is enlightened by the vision of past experiences. He is loved and revered by his family! But he is handicapped by one factor, the nearness of a degree of success that may require a degree of Herculean physical stamina. Dad, I don't want to have to come home to you in a hospital. Please find time to rest each day during the working day.

Mom, yes, Dede is a nut, and I guess I would have laughed, too. I felt that way in college when I lived in her home. Now, can you imagine why I felt I had to move out? She is a great friend but very difficult many times. Then, at eighty-five, maybe she's entitled to it.

About getting the pumpernickel and beef stick roll, yes and no. The food was great. I do appreciate it. For Christmas, what I want is a big fruitcake oozing in rum. I'll even send the rum.

Got another great letter from Brenda. You've really got a gem of a daughter, let alone me having such a great sister.

Well, take excellent care of everything, and let me see some pictures of that garden. I've heard one heck of a lot about it. What did I leave that Polaroid there for, anyhoo?

                                                              Your son

CHAPTER 7

⚜

Tet changed the war with an awful finality, I thought. It marked a change in me, too. I knew that I had been changing. I felt unaware at times, like an igneous rock hardening from hot lava.

The image of the baby stayed with me, haunted me, plagued me with the unholy dishonor of the thing. I wrestled with my own commitment to kill. I had made that commitment, made it for the sake of a cause. So had that VC. But shooting a baby had nothing to do with a military mission. There was a difference. I had to believe there was a difference. And yet I knew, at some level, there wasn't.

No one from my past, my training, my consciousness talked about these things. I knew I wasn't alone in this kind of speculation. But no one talked about it. Everyone seemed alone for a while after Tet, alone with their own thoughts. Alone to find whatever answers they could.

I found none. I found my thoughts scrambled at times. Landing that day back at Sa Dec, I had looked down at the activity of the town and the compound, and for a moment, the people had looked like mice, scurrying about with a frenetic energy. For a second, my eyes lost focus, and the people were mice. And I was back in the classroom, a Boy Scout with curiosity, who hadn't learned contempt. There were mice in the classroom, caged white mice, like in every other tenth-grade science classroom, I supposed. Caged white mice doing what caged white mice do.

It shocked me, shocked all of the class when part of a newly birthed litter, a squirming mass of fascinating, innocent little white bodies, was devoured by other mice in the cage. It probably didn't please Mr. Crane, our teacher, either. But he, the teacher, asked us, "Why, when the mice were so well fed, so well watered and cared for, their cages kept clean, why did some mice eat the newborns?"

Tall and toothy, Mr. Crane confronted the twenty-five of us, who waited for him and for his answers. None of us could explain it, and there was no reply.

"You've seen, class, a basic desire at work here. There is a basic desire for those in the pack to protect what they sense is their own. And it is not only mice. You know now that some animals will kill not only the young of other species, but will kill their own. Male bears have been known to kill their own cubs just to force the female to mate with them again."

We were rapt in the confusion of the event and the explanation. It was not part, I was sure, of the lesson plan. But Mr. Crane tried to bring order into the chaos.

"Now," Mr. Crane went on, "these are animals. Do you think man is capable of this?"

We didn't think so before now.

"Well, what about World War II? Hitler…the Japanese mass murders of Chinese…" Mr. Crane paused.

We agreed.

He paused.

"What about the Americans who killed Indians? Why did we kill?"

We had landed at Sa Dec before I could remember what I had thought about Mr. Crane's questions. Such things had no answers borne of logic.

"Lieutenant! Welcome back, Te We!" It was Private Le.

I was weary, very weary, and very surprised at what I could do. Le looked like a long-lost brother to me. I felt a flood of relief at his smile and his concern about me.

"The VC came down the river," Le said, pointing to the Mekong and smiling.

I understood the reason for the smile. If they had come down the canal, his own home, his paintings, and his life would have been in their path.

Le and I walked toward the headquarters building where I had to check in.

LaRue was waiting for me. He approached me quickly as he saw me enter, smiling, his hand extended in welcome.

"Glad you're back, Pritchard. Good job."

"Thank you, sir," I replied, looking around. "Where is everybody?"

"Out on mop up. It seems that the VC had no idea how close they came to taking Sa Dec. Then, when they lost Vinh Long, they pulled back."

LaRue put a hand on my shoulder, walking me toward the door.

"Paul, I want you to get some rest now. Then we'll need to get some prisoners interrogated. There's a lot of hard feelings. Watch how they handle the prisoners."

There were indeed hard feelings. LaRue was telling me to keep the torture from starting again. I felt an almost uncomfortable twist in my gut. He had used my first name deliberately. He had never done it before. I appreciated it, the personal feeling of it.

"By the way, Paul," he said, stopping at the door, "you did well. The colonel told me to tell you. He wants to congratulate you himself. We're putting you in for a medal. The Vietnamese want to give you one, too." He paused, looking at me closely. "Anyway…for what it's worth."

"Thanks, Major."

Back in the hooch, I repeated the ritual I had begun during my early days in Vietnam, a luxury, a cleansing. I took a long drenching-steaming-deep-breathing-pay-no-attention-to-the-chlorine-smell shower. When I was young, and the Kansas City summers seemed unbearable in those days of no air conditioning, the shower had provided similar relief. So, at scout camp and in college, showers were relaxing moments alone. Now, they had become a more needed event, an inner cleansing, a purification.

And sleep. It was so deep. It was finally restful. My time clock partially restored, I awoke at suppertime.

I ate dinner and headed off to the bar to catch up on the news. The bar was sparse that evening.

"Hey! Lieutenant! I thought you were supposed to bring us some good booze from Saigon!"

"Sorry, guys." I smiled, and it felt good. "I got another assignment."

Everyone seemed to be trying to find a way to recover their humor, their equilibrium. Some found it in clowning, but most seemed to find it in telling stories. There were dozens of them at the bar that evening. Everyone was a hero. Everyone had just missed by "this much" a bullet with his name on it. Some, I think, told stories to fight the fatigue or pace their drink. We all listened to try to get a grasp of what had happened and to whom.

Many of the advisory team had been up for long hours on evening shifts. The NCOs had been doing their day work and night guard duty, as well. The officers had been out in the field every day rather than the usual once or twice a week. Even administrative officers had gone out with the Vietnamese units. We were all confronting a new reality. There would be no more nine-to-five schedules. We were looking at a real war.

Private Le found me. I learned that Faw was fine and that there was no word as yet about Moi. He agreed that she was probably at her family's home at Chau Duc near the Cambodian border. No one knew if they had survived what was intense action.

I walked back to my hooch, thinking that I owed my family a letter and wondering what to say. I sat down to write and stopped, confounded for a moment.

"Dear Mom and Dad," I began. That part was easy. "I'm sure you heard about the Tet offensive." I stopped again, shaping my thoughts and a decision. I had always downplayed the war in my letters. It was honest understatement, though. I didn't lie to them. I used the letters to reassure them, I guess, and to reassure myself in the process. I wrote them carefully. My parents were still very good at reading me; in fact, they could do so better than I could most of the time. But now there was nothing they could do if I needed help, at least the kind of help you can describe in a letter.

Still undecided what to tell them, I took a stroll around the compound with my thoughts. As I walked, my thoughts turned to my scoutmaster. He was a memorable man to me, a good man, a respected surgeon, and dedicated to his three sons and his troop. My father's job required a lot of travel, so I probably landed more questions on Dr. Hodgson than he wanted. Once, probably while suffering with the guilt of some childhood misdeed, I asked him if he ever lied. Had he ever lied to his patients? Weren't there times when a lie was OK, say, when someone was dying?

Dr. Hodgson was usually a man of few words, but he seemed to take very seriously my query.

"I'm sure that there are times when the truth makes no difference. I'm sure that there are times when the truth will add pain to an already painful situation. A lie, on the other hand, might even help a patient or the family sleep better. But, Paul, I always tell the truth, not so much for the patient as for myself. If I begin to tell lies to my patients, I might begin to believe them myself."

He paused, watching for my reaction.

"Besides, Paul, if nothing else, I couldn't remember all the lies I would have to tell!" He jested to lighten the load of his truth.

I walked back to the typewriter, a tool of truth or of lies.

"We were lucky despite what you might have heard." I began again. "The war was all around us in other provinces but with only one difficult night here at Sa Dec."

Accurate so far, I thought. I knew from the reports that Saigon and the other provinces had had tougher times.

"Captain An and I had to return to Vinh Long. It was difficult, but we did our job," I continued.

Bullshit! There it was, staring at me, and it was pure bullshit. I had told them the truth and left out the heart of it. Telling the truth, I decided, was much like peeling an onion: a delicate job with a price in tears. I didn't think I was ready to pay it. I wasn't sure that the inner part had any greater value than the outer. I wadded up the letter and pitched it over my shoulder. And started again.

"Dear Mom and Dad,

"I'm sure you have heard much about the Tet offensive. It was tough, even though Sa Dec survived. Captain An and I were sent down the river road to join in the recapture of Vinh Long.

"I must tell you that we did not face the same VC as we had in the past. These were from North Vietnam. They were well-trained fighters, committed. Before, we faced guerilla forces with little staying power. The Tet Viet Cong had commitment, supplies, and objectives.

"This war has many subwars within it, Mom and Dad, and it has many subthemes."

I felt myself sliding, moving into the onion again. I got back to the facts.

> "Sa Dec was attacked from the north. The VC unit was modest, and we were lucky that our Vietnamese troops were together at a party at a location between the VC and the compound. They did well."

That's enough, I thought. They were intelligent. I did not have to describe things better left out. I added a few concerns and signed off, sealed the letter, and added the word "free" to the upper right-hand corner of the envelope.

I walked out of the hooch and dropped it in the box in the headquarters building, aware of the irony. Soldiers don't have to put up the price of a postage stamp to send a letter home. It was encouragement to do so, clear and simple. But the cost of writing home was more than the cost of the stamp. It was the cost of honesty, of concern, of peeling an onion.

It did not take long for Sa Dec to settle down: more than a day, but less than a week. I realized this early in the evening of my second day back from the *Benowah,* walking down the hardened gravel road that led to the point of the compound. I was tired but feeling a kind of comfort in the familiarity of being on my own turf, being able to sleep in my own bunk, being able to take a hot shower, to wear clean clothes. It was measured in small pleasures, but it was very real.

Men were walking into and out of their hooches, returning from their day's activities, settling into a schedule like that of before Tet. Their movements seemed so normal to me—like the end of the office day anywhere. It struck me that it had been a strange war indeed before Tet, with office hours, a hot shower, and some comfort.

Now, the concrete tennis-and-basketball court was filled with men in fatigue pants, boots, and no shirts, building up a sweat in a pickup basketball game. I waved at a few and stopped to watch. From the common building on the other side of the court came the sound of ping pong. Things were getting back to "normal," and that was the joke. War is a game of chaos played by men who seek order.

It was almost like before Tet, when there was some predictability, some normality. That seemed to be what everyone wanted—all of the Americans, anyway. And we returned to those normal comforts as quickly as we could.

I walked over to the club, which had finally received sufficient alcoholic supplies to make my entrance less than another kind of joke. It wasn't as ordered, but it kept them pacified.

The club was not like those I had encountered in training. It was open to all of us, part of the great equalizing of a war. Rank was not the criterion here. Just survival and some degree of competence, I guess. Those were the tickets to the club and to some respect and credibility in a war zone.

As I walked in, Lieutenant Colonel Turnage was walking out the door with his first lieutenant, Lieutenant Simon. I knew Simon slightly, liked him, and wondered just how he got on with "Uptight Turnage." Simon had been a real help to me and to Lip in our first days at Sa Dec, a short fellow, lively, friendly, and supportive.

"Good evening, Lieutenant," Turnage said in official greeting that required an official response but implied no interest in me. I was "Paul" to most everyone else after Tet but not to Turnage.

Lieutenant Simon greeted me in the same way. I did my duty and headed in the door of the club, wondering what had gotten into him. He was not usually so aloof.

I was greeted with the usual round of pleasantries, now that at least some of the booze had arrived, and with a few hero hails. A "welcome home" here, a "good job" there, a few nontraditional pleasantries from the corner. It felt good.

"Well, Lieutenant," Sergeant Wilson greeted me from behind the bar, where usually there were two Vietnamese employees. "I'm all you've got, so what'll it be? And it better be Pabst Blue Ribbon. By the way, the first one's on me. Good work, Lieutenant."

"Thanks, Sarge. What's with the bar routine? Where are the Coes?" I asked.

"New orders, sir!" he replied. "Colonel Turnage orders, sir! New security rules"—he paused—"until Colonel Calnan gets back."

His point was unmistakable. At one time or another, we all referred to Turnage as a skinhead. That was what we called every uptight senior officer. It took some doing to earn that title if, like Turnage, you were in the army.

"Join me, Paul. Have a chair." I was invited by Captain Boston, our own Plato on the advisory team. I joined him.

"How did it go in Vinh Long?" he asked.

I recounted the story, some of it anyway, what he needed to hear. He listened, interrupting occasionally, asking questions, good questions, chin in palm, in the manner that had earned him his nickname. That and the fact that Boston was the compound administrative officer, responsible for seeing that the team was functioning, the one who stayed behind, and generally the fount of all knowledge.

"Where's the colonel?" I queried, not without a little concern. I felt as Sergeant Wilson did about Turnage.

Boston shrugged. "Bough's in Saigon. Helping Westmoreland outsmart the VC, I suppose. Actually, I gather our good luck impressed the Saigon boys. Anyway, they pulled him up and put Turnage in charge here."

He leaned forward, lowering his voice.

"And that's the problem, Paul. He's acting like he's the senior advisor. Thinks he's going to keep the job."

I sighed.

"And check this!" Boston went on, glancing around him and concluding it was all right to continue. "Turnage put Simon in for a Medal of Honor. Simon and his ARNVs followed some VC company and took them on with hand-to-hand combat. It was an all-night battle. You'd think that Simon was John Wayne! You should hear Simon brag to the rest of the team!"

So that explained Turnage and Simon. I was impressed though. It was seldom that any of the advisors had engaged the VC in a traditional battle of that kind.

"Well, I guess Simon does have something to be proud of," I offered, not without some reverence, picturing what it must have been like.

"Yeah." Boston grimaced and waved the comment aside. "Yeah, I suppose. But some of the NCOs tell me that Simon's pressure led to the loss of twelve

Vietnamese. They say Turnage pushed him to do it and that the Vietnamese are good and pissed at both of them for forcing the fight."

That figured, I thought, and sighed again, wondering what Captain An would say about this. There was silence of savoring the truth about those who fight to be heros, for vanity.

"How did the rest of the provinces do?" I asked Boston.

He settled back into his chair. "Most of the provinces pulled through. Even An Giang got hit, but the local people controlled it."

An Giang was the province that was always the exception in the region. Everybody who lived there was part of a religious sect that hated the VC and did pretty well by themselves, keeping the VC out of their area.

"The only real surprise was the Special Forces team at Cu Duc." He continued, "They got hit and couldn't find one member. I hear he had gone into town to visit his girlfriend. Must have been pretty confident that Tet was going to be a party! Sure wasn't a party for him. The team found him the next day. His girlfriend must have been VC, or maybe they got to her. Who knows? Anyway, they think he'd been tortured. They put a grenade under him after they tortured him and just blew him in half. It was pretty bad."

Maybe it was that my beer was getting warm, but it suddenly started to go down very bitterly. My stomach churned as I flashed on the possibility that that could have been me. It could have been Moi.

"Goddammit!"

I startled Boston.

"This damn war! Just too many loose ends! Too many guys trying to be John Wayne! Too many trying to act like there isn't any war."

Boston looked on, surprised. I took a long swig of the now-bitter beer, deciding that I was going to stay right here. No mess hall tonight. I was going to have a few more beers. I left the table and brought back two more.

"Here, Plato." I handed him his beer. "How about a toast to this fucking war? Cheers."

"Paul…hang on, Paul."

"Jesus, Plato! Look at it! It's a joke! Look at you. How the hell can you administer a goddamn war? Well?"

"Paul...I..."

"You try to move things here, people there, supplies in, but how do you administer death and fucking heroism? It's a total loss of sanity. It's men and women and babies, for Christ's sake. How do you fucking administer that? And guys trying to be heroes with other people's lives?"

I stopped. "Sorry, Plato. It's not you, buddy. It's this goddamn war."

"I know, Paul." Boston reached out, his hand now on my shoulder.

"Read my report on Turnage last fall. Read how he pushed the ARVN. He didn't care about the war. He wanted action! War, death, body counts! Plato, I told LaRue about it, you know. He's not an advisor; he's John Wayne—but this is no make-believe movie!"

"Yeah, I read it, Paul. So did Colonel Bough. He talked to Turnage about it."

"And just what difference did it make?"

"I don't know," Plato replied, finishing off his beer.

Dear Brenda and the Gang,

First of all, many thanks for the very illustrative letter on silk. I do appreciate it. I know it will help me find some things that I have been trying to buy but have been concerned about the quality.

I am a little concerned right now about the mail situation. I have received many letters from home during the past two weeks, and all of them state that they have received not a letter from me. I was unable to write for a time because I was in Saigon in school and had neither the time nor the facilities to write. It was one long week, classwork from six thirty in the morning to six thirty at night. What makes Saigon so difficult is that there is the normal tension of the bustling big city-its dirt, its gaseous atmosphere-permeated by the sounds of interaction of people at war, machines of war, and fear. It sounds like New York until you add the magic ingredient of war. War only adds to its many already obnoxious factors.

While we were there, the Chinese embassy was attacked in broad daylight, and the sound of the attack from my position only a few blocks away made me aware of the environment. Later, one of my classmates and I were driving through town when something crashed into our jeep. My friend who was driving stopped his car and slammed it into reverse as if he were in the States and trying to see the kid who threw the rock. I looked at him and was appalled. In the delta, if an object were thrown at a jeep, the instinctive thing to do would be to haul out of there. I asked him if he thought about what he was doing, and he realized how stupid it was. Fortunately, it was only a flashlight battery. Fortunately because he rolled back over it and sat there looking for the culprit.

You come to a point when you wonder about your very purpose over here. If you have a chance to read the article in the October 9 issue of Newsweek, which was banned in Vietnam, the article on page twenty, "Their Lions, Our Rabbits," well, you'll be reading the gospel. To add to its realism, you might notice the shoulder patches of the men in the picture, which are the same as my bunch of boys. This has been an experience beyond external understanding. There is a stench of rotten politics (for example, the G2 for the ARVN is now under house arrest because he used intelligence funds for his own purposes). I learned a few days ago that he will still get his promotion because, as my ARVN friend informed me, "He comes from a very wealthy family." Well, I was the guy who reported him to the Vietnamese police. I don't go downtown because my hide might not make it. On the other hand, it would only incriminate him, so I doubt if he would do anything. But to add to the insult, the guy is soon to join the big-time staff in Saigon. Their emphasis on tact and respect is more obsequious so as not to step on toes. They sacrifice the success of what would seem to us the main purpose of all their activity. In other words, they may die from Charlie overrunning their headquarters, but at least they won't have offended the guy who was supposed to keep up the security. Bitter? Yes, but mostly frustrated.

One of the best uplifts for me is to read Mom and Dad's pride and love for the fine times that you all are sharing with them. Never before have I seen such harmony in our family. Brenda, you are a blessing as a mother to your kids, a daughter to our parents, and as my great sister. No woman can do more than that except to include a wife. And I can't see how a husband could ask for his wife to be more. Tell Bill that! Ha! Take excellent care of that group. I can't wait to get back.

Love,
Your brother Paul

CHAPTER 8

⚜

I stood in front of Captain Boston's desk in the administrative building and relished every one of his words.

"Well, Paul, you've got the next R&R to Taiwan. This is your R&R, buddy. The colonel told me before he left for Saigon that you deserved it, too."

"Thanks, Plato."

I knew it was Plato who had recommended that I get it. He knew I needed it. But it was nice to hear that Colonel Bough thought it was deserved.

"You sure they're going to let me out of the country?" I asked. Things were pretty much back to normal around the compound, but Tet had certainly introduced a new element of uncertainty.

"Shit, Paul! This war will be won or lost with or without you!" He laughed. "Get your bag packed, and catch the next chopper out. I've got one coming in the day after tomorrow. You're either on it, or we'll put you in Cambodia with the VC for your next duty."

We both smiled. His smile was in jest; mine was in relief.

The possible rest and recuperation destinations included Manila, Singapore, Bangkok, Tokyo, Honolulu, Sydney, and Taipei. I had made the R&R choice some time before, and it was a difficult one. I knew all the married soldiers would be trying for Honolulu so they could meet their wives there. I figured that I would see Honolulu and probably Tokyo at some time in my life. I had, though, suggested to Libba that she meet me in Honolulu and, to my surprise, she agreed. But the plans never got together. She would have to purchase a ticket long in advance, and I would never know until the last minute whether I could get there.

So, after our attempt at coordination fell through, I picked Taipei. I had long been intrigued by the mystique of this island and the story of Chiang Kai-shek. And it was unlikely that I would make it there again.

I spent the next day making plans and getting organized for all the "get-mes." I decided to try to call home and Libba. If luck were with me, I could talk to my parents and Libba about any gifts.

It was a great joke, the compound's telephone. You had to yell to be heard. Everything had to be followed by "over" and "out." There were always two operators on the line, so nothing personal could be discussed without some embarrassment. The married men could be heard around the compound shouting to their wives that they were fine and healthy and that all was well, closing with, "I love you, honey. Over."

Then there were the get-mes. Whenever someone was heading out of country, it was an open invitation to everybody else to ask for things to be brought back. Lieutenant Blair wanted jade.

"I've got a piece from everyplace around here," he explained, "except Taiwan."

"Are you sure jade is natural to Taiwan?" I asked, rather bemused as my get-me list grew.

He paused and frowned in what seemed to be ignorance exposed. "Well, if they sell it there, and they say it's Taiwan jade, buy me some."

The war seemed more like a scavenger hunt for some than a search for personal purpose. I thought about this on occasion and wondered if it were a kind of mental escape, a building of the security of possessions in the insecurity of war. It was probably just the same impulse to collect. People collect coins and stamps in normal times. Here, they collected weapons, VC items, and some object from each country they visited.

The most surprising get-me came from Lieutenant Wa. "My friend," he said, isolating me at the bar the night before I left, "I have special request for General. General wants you to bring back BB gun. It is not for General," he assured me. "It is for General's son."

The request was an ironic one, to say the least. I didn't know the boy but had seen him at a distance a few times. I could picture him pestering his father, who daily worried about the weapons for his division. I wondered if the general smiled at the thought of trying to figure out how to locate a BB gun to satisfy his son. I wondered if he thought of it as a weapon. Probably not.

But I did. I remembered the Black Beauty that my parents had given me for my twelfth birthday. I remembered it as a symbol of their trust in me. In that sense, it was more than a weapon; it was a rite of maturation. But in the end it was just another weapon to me. Once as a kid I went out with a buddy on my grandmother's farm—two small warriors stalking an undefined prey. I saw a bird on a post in the shadow of a tree. I aimed my BB gun and fired. It fell. My buddy was impressed, and I was quite proud of this success until I walked up to the place where the bird had fallen. It was a red-winged blackbird, my grandmother's favorite bird. It was still alive, twitching, fighting a death that was more painful for me, I know. I suddenly wanted to take it all back. But I was stricken with recognition that killing was something you couldn't take back.

I asked Plato about bringing back a BB gun, hoping there would be some rule or regulation to prohibit this. It would have been typical to have some regulation to stop you from bringing a BB gun into a war zone. Plato laughed and said that it was all right, and I put it on the list.

"Typical. When you want the regs to stop you, they are never there," I joked.

He replied, "Maybe it's a first. You get to write the reg."

The chopper lifted me up and away from the compound whose denizens- Advisors, Vietnamese soldiers, workers--had grown more and more nervous after Tet. It grew smaller and smaller, finally disappearing into the landscape. The aftermath of Tet was ever present as we flew toward Saigon. Smudges of burned-out buildings littered the countryside. The popular forces troops' small compounds looked charred and in need of repairs even from above.

Saigon looked marred, different from how it had appeared to me in my convoy visits before Tet. There were shattered and cratered buildings in the suburban areas of the sprawling capital. But it was the people who were different.

Saigon pre-Tet had a casual pace, occasional smiles, and a sense of economic bustle of a war remote from daily life. Now, people moved faster. They had weary expressions. Saigon looked and felt nothing like it did before Tet.

The American troops in Saigon had changed, too. Their bunkers and guard buildings had been made of wood and metal before Tet. Now they were made of mounds of sandbags. Soldiers wore full battle gear, from steel pots to flak jackets. I saw only a few out without their rifles, and all seemed alert.

The R&R processing center was different from what I had heard. The usual "hurry up and wait" attitude was gone. It was quick and very businesslike. It seemed that Tet had made its point to these men, too. They worked as though they believed that the quicker they did their work, the faster their time in country would pass and the sooner they would be home.

I had just a short time to kill before the plane took off, so I decided to wander over to the Base Exchange at Tan Son Nhut airfield. Blackened planes still littered the runway at Tan Son Nhut, though there looked to be an armada of new ones on the field, all under heavy guard.

A bus took me to the Base Exchange, a big diesel-powered monster driven by a Vietnamese who hardly seemed big enough for the task. There were few conversations on the bus, even among people who seemed to be intentionally sitting together, all by the exit. The bus windows were open but covered with a heavy wire screen, apparently to keep out grenades or bombs thrown at it. Now there was a classic technical solution, I thought, that worsened the problem rather than solved it. A bomb might well bounce off the screen, but if one hooked on the screen, it would blow off every head inside.

The Base Exchange was bizarrely like a suburban shopping center at home. People were streaming in and out, and as I joined them, I found myself forgetting where I was, forgetting the war, feeling like I was back in the States. Shopping was a sort of martini.

Once inside, there were only a few women shoppers. Everyone wore green fatigues. I was quickly distracted, however. Behind the counters were some of the most beautiful women I had seen in a long time. The women were Korean and it seemed that Koreans were running all of the commercial enterprises on the Base Exchange. Several were gorgeous. I caught myself staring more than once as I shopped. I found myself busily comparing these women to Moi and to the few American women.

Since I had little time, I took the bus back to the R&R processing center to change into street clothes for the flight to Taipei.

Everyone seemed to loosen up and relax as we put on our street clothes for the trip. We had all been too long in the dismal green fatigues that hung like tired balloons in the humid weather.

It was easy to continue feeling relaxed on the plane. It was a contract commercial jet from the States that took off in an immediate and jarring ascent. Saigon was still fighting the war, and the pilot obviously wanted to avoid the possibility of sniper fire.

There was brilliance in Charlie's tactics. He was so good at catching everyone when they least expected it. We, Charlie's enemies, had to be in a constant state of tension and fear. And when we relaxed, when we had a sense of things being under control, lulled into a sense of security, like on this plane, there would be Charlie, who had waited patiently, quietly, for just that moment to strike again.

I had been taught that surprise was the singular element in a guerrilla war. *Maybe so*, I decided, *but not in this war*. The key was patience. The example in ROTC class of a guerrilla warrior was the American Revolutionary War soldier who was adept at surprise tactics because he, unlike his British adversary, knew the countryside. But here, both the VC and the South Vietnamese soldiers knew the countryside. Surprise was difficult, although Tet had demonstrated that it was possible. Success really depended more on patience, THE virtue of the Orient. It depended on the waiting, not on knowing which tree might hide a soldier.

"Where you from?"

The ubiquitous introductory comment of this war or any other, I suppose, came from my right. He looked like he belonged in high school.

I paused for a moment, not knowing whether to answer with my hometown or my Vietnam assignment.

"Kansas City," I said. "How about you?"

"Philly. I'm with the Big Red One now. You?"

"I'm a recon company advisor in Four Corps."

"Advisor?" he asked, surprised. "You an officer?"

"Second lieutenant."

Everybody on the plane was dressed in similar street clothes. There were only the smallest details to distinguish one from another, to pick out rank. Most of us had lived in country for months, so the distinctions were even less pronounced, because we all bought our civilian clothes at the Base Exchange on military posts.

"How'd you do in Tet?" the young soldier asked.

"We made it," I replied, "but we were lucky." I told him the story of the Tet party for the Vietnamese soldiers and how it had probably saved the compound from a successful attack.

"We got it from every direction." He seemed awed with the memory of it. "Charlie had those new Russian rockets. Boy, they really had us targeted. Must have had some great spotters. I was on HQ night duty, and after the first rounds, they really opened up. Real pros. Don't waste nothing."

He shook his head, looking at the floor.

The man on my left had sat quietly through this conversation. "We got it pretty bad, too," he said calmly.

What happened to you?" I asked, turning in my seat.

"They came at us in Saigon from every direction. They were all over the back alleys, avoiding the main streets where the ARVN had their tanks. Charlie is not stupid, I'll tell you that. He knew just where all the bigshots lived and avoided all the troops. You know, they never told us at HQ how bad we got hit, but when I saw all those planes blown up at Tan Son Nhut, I figured Charlie had to have been inside the perimeter."

"Looks that way," I agreed.

He adjusted his seat back and settled in a partial recline.

"Glad I'm up here," he said before closing his eyes.

We landed in Taipei in the dark with little visible except glistening city lights in the distance. I could just make out hills, steep ones, above the glow of the city.

The Chinese immigration officers surprised me. They were as big as we were. They waved us through the gates without the slightest concern. American troops moving through meant only one thing. Every moment the troops spent away from the shops meant less purchasing.

I grabbed my bag and followed the flow into a room furnished in classic military style, gray, complete with metal folding chairs and two US military police standing at the front of the room.

An officer moved up to join them.

"Men, I'm Lieutenant Packer. You are guests of the Taiwanese people. Don't forget it. Don't abuse this privilege. You are in their country. You are subject to their rules. They have a curfew. They frown on drunkenness. It's a sure way to get back to Nam on a fast plane."

Packer clearly knew this script well.

"If you have any drugs," he continued in the tone of an incantation, "they will keep you here forever. About women: the hotel girls are under a pretty tight medical watch. But you are advised to use your head."

That brought a laugh. Packer smiled at his own joke, probably used in every one of these briefings.

"A final word. Don't miss your flight back. We haven't lost anybody yet. Questions?"

There were questions about limits on purchases and whether Beitou was off-limits. I hadn't heard about this place.

"No, it's not off limits, but watch yourself. And be careful. The Japanese men still think it's their turf."

As the briefing ended, it was apparent that several groups of GIs knew exactly what they wanted and where to get it. They hustled together through the hotel desk lines in complete control.

I got in line in front of the China Palace Hotel desk along with another officer, and when our check-ins were complete, we headed for the bus that would drop all of us off.

"Been here before?" I asked.

"Third trip." He wore a huge grin and spoke slowly, relaxed. "I found this beautiful Taiwanese girl. She asked me to come back. We fell in love. We write. Actually, she has a friend do the writing. She's waiting for me at the hotel."

I got on the bus and sat through the late-night ride with a hollow sort of feeling. It was late. I was tired. No one was there to greet me. All I knew about the place was what I read in the guidebook I had bought.

The China Palace looked like an average high-rise hotel of about ten stories, though it seemed to be nicer than some of the other hotels we had passed. The lobby was like any lobby in the States, except perhaps that check-in was quicker and more efficient. The bellmen wore smiles and swarmed on our baggage.

My newfound friend was in a state of euphoria as we checked in. He registered first and started to lope off in the direction of the elevators, stopped, and returned.

"Meet us in the bar on the top floor," he said, extending his hand. "I'm Sawyer."

"Pritchard. Will do." I shook his hand, and he roared back to the elevators.

A bellhop approached me. "You visit Taipei before, sir?"

"First time."

"Good. You have good time. Mr. Wu come soon."

I hardly listened to him. I wanted to check in, shower, and get up to the bar to meet Sawyer and this beautiful girl.

The bellhop showed me to my room, repeatedly assuring me of what a wonderful time I would have. We walked into my room and were immediately followed in by a middle-aged Chinese man in a black business suit, carrying a large book under his arm.

"Welcome to Taipei, Lieutenant."

I was startled for a moment. He had to have read the hotel register.

"My name is Mr. Wu. I will provide trips and hostesses. I can tell you where to buy gifts. Please call me on your telephone at this number," he said, handing me a card.

So this was the promised host. I told him I would get back to him if I needed him.

Undaunted, Mr. Wu pulled out the book.

"For tonight, I have many pretty hostesses."

He flipped the pages, inviting me to look. It was a portfolio of young-looking Chinese women. They were all smiling.

"Not tonight. Thanks."

Call me, Lieutenant," said Mr. Wu, with a slight tilt of his head. "I am your friend, Lieutenant." He backed out the door, still smiling.

I cleaned up and headed immediately for the bar on the tenth floor. Sawyer was already there, talking seriously with the bartender, when he saw me enter.

"Pritchard! She's gone! Sawyer was in some distress as I took the seat next to his. "She's gone! Something about her family, he says." Sawyer pointed in the direction of the bartender. "Bullshit! She's with some other GI or one of those Japanese businessmen."

"Let me buy you a beer," I offered. "You have her phone number?"

"No, only her address," he replied in a subdued voice.

"Tell you what, Sawyer, why don't we get out and see the country tomorrow? Maybe she'll be here tomorrow night when we get back. They open the bar at four."

Sawyer stared at the liquor bottles on the wall while we drank. He said nothing. I finished my bottle and excused myself.

I slept well that night, ordered a western omelet in the morning, and read some more of the tourist literature as I ate. I called Sawyer, but the hotel desk clerk said he had left early.

The museum. I had been well-trained. My mother had always taken me to art galleries when I was young, whether I wanted to go or not. So I decided to spend the day at the National Palace Museum. The tour book had said that it was a beautiful drive through the pastoral countryside to a national museum in a mountain with more collections than one could see in a lifetime.

And true it was. The museum was built right into the side of a mountain. It was a spectacular sight and a necessity, I was told by the tour guide who led the small group of tourists up the grand steps leading to the museum's entrance. It was essential, he assured us, to protect the almost countless artifacts and treasures of China's past from "a mainland invasion by the Communist bandits."

It was my first taste of the real paranoid fear in Taiwan that the Communist bandits from the mainland would invade any day. It was a fear that had proved unfounded in the twenty years since the Chinese Revolution, but it seemed to be an everyday reality in Taipei. Paranoia, I decided, is essential for many military governments in order to avoid complacency and to maintain the flow of US aid for military control of the island.

I called for Sawyer again as soon as I got back to the hotel, but there was no answer. Figuring that the bar would be a likely place to check, I went up to the tenth floor. Sure enough, there was Sawyer.

"How'd you do today?" he asked without much interest and a particularly forlorn expression on his face.

"Not bad. I got some rest and saw the national museum. How about you? What did you do?"

"I tried everything! I tried to find her home, but nobody around here seemed to know her. Or they wouldn't tell me where she lives, anyway. The address I have is some uncle. He was no help." Sawyer gulped his beer. "He has a store. If I wasn't going to buy something, he wasn't going to answer my questions. Anyway, I only had the damn cab driver to translate. Who knows what he was saying."

I had my beer by now. I was listening to Sawyer, but I was tired and hungry.

"Look," I said, "let's go get some Mongolian barbecue. I heard about a place from some Australians on the tour today. They said it's great. Then we can come back here and see what's happening."

"I don't know…" Sawyer began hesitantly. Half of him wanted to go. "Maybe she'll be here tonight. Maybe her uncle told her I was here. I'm not sure I want to leave."

"Sawyer," I tried again, "look, if you went to her uncle's house, she probably knows you're here. If she wanted to see you, she would have called."

Sawyer looked at me with a pained expression.

"You're going to spend every cent you have on cabs and beer. Come on. I'll buy dinner."

Sawyer was quiet for a while. Both of us drank our beer, while I waited. Finally, he turned to me and gave my arm a light punch.

"You're on! Let's go. You're right, too. Shit, you know, I met her the first night I was here. I haven't seen anything around here."

We ate that night in a rooftop restaurant in a hotel not far from ours. It was full of people, and the barbecue was an experience with big Chinese men stir-frying over a fire anything you chose from a long line of food. The night was cool and the atmosphere relaxed. I think it did both of us good.

We were finishing off the evening, watching the people, drinking a few more beers when I saw a vaguely familiar man moving toward our table.

"Nice to see both of you here, Lieutenants." It was Mr. Wu with company. "I brought two of my friends." He smiled broadly and introduced us. "This is Miss Chew and this is Miss Wang."

Both women smiled with some embarrassment as Mr. Wu seated them at the table.

"They are not busy, gentlemen." Mr. Wu continued, "If you would like, they will be your hostesses. You do not need to pay them if you do not wish. Please, be my guest."

I looked at Sawyer and surveyed the scene. Miss Wang, seated next to me, was quite pretty. She was dressed in a tight skirt slit up the side and a light blue blouse embroidered with flowers across the shoulder.

"You like Taipei?" she asked, smiling at me.

"Yes, I like Taipei," I replied. This was going to be shallow conversation. But what the hell.

"You like to dance?" she inquired.

I looked over at Sawyer, who was engaged in a similar conversation, before answering.

"Yes."

"Good!" Miss Wang announced. "We go to my friend's bar."

"No. We stay here," I said firmly, not waiting for Sawyer's opinion.

"OK." Her agreement was quick, and it surprised me.

"Hey, what the hell, Paul," Sawyer interrupted. "My girl isn't coming back. And if she does, maybe this will get her jealous. Let's go."

We were back at the hotel and in the bar in no time. We danced in the darkness of the lounge with other similar couples of lonesome GIs and Chinese women. Miss Wang knew how to dance and gently rub her soft body against mine. I liked the attention. Simple pleasures.

We sat down to our drinks. Hers was a cocktail that looked like little more than a five-dollar glass of weak tea. We watched the dance floor for a few minutes before realizing that Sawyer and his companion were gone. Miss Wang smiled. We both knew what was next.

"I go with you to your room," she said, less a question than a statement of understanding.

I nodded. It was a nighttime of needs.

She left my room in the night. But not before waking me enough to whisper that I should ask Mr. Wu to bring her back, that she "loved" me. It was a job for her, one I deeply appreciated. I went back to sleep.

It was Sawyer who woke me, his voice cheerful and enthusiastic over the telephone.

"Let's get out and see the town, Pritchard. What do you say? I want to get some jewelry for Miss Chew. I'm going to see her tonight."

Soon we were on the streets and in the Western-style shops, buying indiscriminately. We wandered from shop to shop, buying gifts, drawings, a chess set, hand-tailored suits.

When I returned to my room and unloaded the gifts, I sat down to think about what I would do with myself and the time. I had a beer sent up.

"You want to see Mr. Wu?" the waiter asked as he set down the tray.

"Not right now." Everyone, it seemed, worked for Mr. Wu.

The telephone rang before I could get to the beer. I picked it up with some reluctance. I really didn't want to talk to Mr. Wu at that moment. And I was a little tired of Sawyer.

"Lieutenant Pritchard?" It was an American-sounding voice. "I'm Lieutenant Commander Jordan. I just got into town. Got a message from my son. How about dinner tonight?"

I had to think a moment. Jordan, one of my fellow officers at Sa Dec, had said something to me about calling his father, a Navy officer posted in Taipei. I hadn't really expected him to do it, and I never expected to have his father track me down.

"Sounds great, sir. I've got a friend here. May I bring him?"

"Sure, Lieutenant. We're going to Madame Chiang's for dinner. Bring anyone you want. See you at seven."

I was surprised for a moment by the brevity of the whole interchange. It was, though, just like a military man to issue an invitation like it was a radio message. Short and to the point.

Sawyer was, of course, busy with Miss Chew and didn't want to go.

"Be careful, buddy," I said, knowing that warnings would be of no use whatsoever. "Good luck."

When I came down to the lobby, Commander Jordan was waiting for me.

"Welcome to Taipei, Paul. I understand from my son that you're one hell of a soldier. Good to meet you."

He showed me to a Japanese-made sedan parked in front of the hotel. We wended our way through the Taipei traffic, and he asked the questions. I told him about his son, Sa Dec, Tet, about the trip to Taipei, the gift purchases, the museum.

"You know, Paul, I love this country," he said when his questions seemed exhausted for the moment. "The Chinese know how to run a tight ship. This is my second tour. When I came back, it was like I was a returning hero. I even brought back a horizontal freezer for one of my friends."

I looked puzzled.

He smiled and explained, "He's Chinese, and they use those things like coffins here to store the old granny when she dies so that they can bury her at the right time. Here we are," he said, pointing toward a hotel. "This is the Golden Palace. Madame Chiang's hotel. I run the base commissary system here, Paul. We're having dinner with one of my suppliers. They're buying. Food should be spectacular."

Three Chinese men were sitting at the table when we arrived, all dressed in Western-style suits and slicked-back hairstyles. Dinner, though, was anything but Western. Dinner was a feast of many dishes that included shark fin soup, painstakingly colored and stirred so that as the waiter lifted the top of the soup tureen, the soup displayed a perfect yin-yang symbol for just that moment before it was served. There were a number of dishes I didn't bother to have translated. The chicken feet had been enough for me. One of the Chinese men must have caught my look at those. He explained, much to his colleague's amusement, a process of putting live chickens in a hot skillet. Commander Jordan was quite right. The dinner had a bizarre menu, cordial chat, and supreme service.

"Why don't you plan on coming out to my place tomorrow, Paul?" Jordan invited me as he drove me back to the hotel. "At least you can spend your last two days in a real home. Mrs. Lee will take good care of you."

I agreed readily, and we set a time to meet. I stopped by the bar on my way to my room. Sawyer wasn't there, which didn't surprise me. When I got to my room, I didn't get a call from Mr. Wu, which did surprise me.

With a half day to kill, I did some more sightseeing—this time at a village of native Taiwanese whose dress reminded me more of Native American Indians than of anything Chinese, colorful blanket robes, feather caps and leather shoes.

On the way back to the hotel, I wanted exercise and a break from the tour group, so I had the bus driver drop me off. It was a pleasant walk through a park full of ordinary Chinese people doing ordinary things. I stopped to watch a group of young boys playing baseball, and they quickly did the same. They stopped playing and started watching me, talking among themselves.

They seemed to come to some sort of decision in their huddle and started running toward me. They were friendly, shy, bemused.

"Mister, baseball play? Mister, play baseball now?"

Their smiles and fractured English made me smile. It was the first good humor of the whole trip. I also knew what was happening. I had read in the paper that there was an American baseball team in Taipei, and they were probably assuming I was one of them. The truth? It didn't matter at the moment.

I smiled and held out my hand for their ball and a bat. I fanned them out to the field. They ran, cheering in excitement about playing with a real baseball player.

I hit a gentle fly ball to centerfield, my left-handed hit a novelty to the boys. They smiled some more. I needed this.

Sawyer was still nowhere around the hotel when I got back. I worried about him as I packed up. Sawyer seemed to want something desperately, something that wasn't really there. Soldiers learn how to dominate, not share. And in a place like this, we soldiers were viewed simply as sources of income. Sawyer was looking for a companion. But to these people, he was simply prey.

Commander Jordan's house was in the foothills, outside Taipei proper, in a nice neighborhood that seemed quiet, cool, and breezy. It was pleasant, a bachelor's pad, and Mrs. Lee, the housekeeper, knew how to cook American food.

"She worked for me in the Exchange," Jordan explained. "She made hamburgers in the fast-food service. I had to retrain her. Greasiest damn food you've ever seen. I didn't know that was the way they served it in the hamburger shop! Anyhow, she's great now."

We had a few beers, and the conversation turned to Vietnam.

"That is one stupid war," Jordan announced. "I was there for one tour. You'd think we were looking to build a parking lot for California. Why the hell else would we be there? I've never seen such waste. We're paying triple for that war, and the Japanese are getting rich."

"The Japanese?" I didn't have that figured.

"Listen, Paul, the Japanese love us. Believe me! If you look at their recent history, their economy has boomed off the goddamn chart three times. After the big one, during Korea, and now, with Vietnam. There isn't an Asian in the Orient who can understand why we buy everything we do from Japan. They're winning World War II, and we're on their side!"

I knew he was right, but I resented the truth.

"Why are we so damn stupid to be in Vietnam?" I asked.

Jordan looked thoughtful, then just as frustrated as I felt. "I don't know, Paul. Let's hit the sack. We're going to Beitou tomorrow."

A solitary bird woke me the next morning, its chirp a welcome wake-up call. We ate eggs and bacon and drove to Beitou, that place I remembered was discussed in my entry briefing, not quite forbidden but attached with warnings.

Beitou was some distance from Jordan's home. The drive was a pleasant one though, from his suburb, through Taipei, and into the suburbs again, then the outreaches of the city, and through quite rural scenery into the steep hills that surround the Taipei area.

Jordan knew where to go. He had clearly been here before. We drove to a hotel, nestled in the hills, outside the little village of Beitou. It was surrounded by trees at the end of a winding drive along a small river. Once inside, we were greeted by a hostess, who bowed and greeted the commander by name and then led us up a flight of stairs to separate rooms.

"Take it easy, Pritchard," said Jordan as he entered his room. "See you for dinner at six o'clock."

My room was spacious and airy. I stepped out onto the balcony, watching some clouds bunch up around the tops of the higher hills. A knock on my door was followed by the entrance of an entourage of six young women led by an elderly hostess.

"Which would you like?"

I was momentarily floored. I chose.

The afternoon was consumed with a very hot bath, a gentle massage, and the delicacies of total submission: she to my sensual needs, me to her preoccupation with me. We napped in the late afternoon and ordered tea. There was another knock at the door. Jordan, this time.

He stuck his head in the door to query, "Everything OK?"

"Roger," I replied. "Ready when you are. But I'm in no rush." I smiled.

"Great. Let's spend the night."

We ordered dinner, and I amused my companion with my left-handed chopstick action. I looked at her, a lovely woman with gentle features and a penetrating perception of what I needed. It was more than sensual. I needed to feel like I wasn't being used, wasn't prey. I understood Sawyer. All my philosophizing, and here I was. The difference between Sawyer and me was only a matter of degree.

Nam waited only a day away. I wanted to forget it.

Dear Mom and Dad,

I'm sitting in the airport at Tan Son Nhut airfield on the outskirts of Saigon, waiting for a flight to Sa Dec. You could understand how long I've waited when I say that I finished one book, two magazines, and two newspapers (nine till four so far).

I had a nice conversation with one of our sergeants and then two VN officers, one a doctor. We talked about the war, medical school, the cost of living. The doctor went to medical school for eight years in Saigon. It costs about ten dollars for your tuition to go to the university here. The school of medicine was originally taught in French, which was obviously more of a prohibitive factor than the tuition. But now it takes Vietnamese, French, and English.

Their medical company has been in I Corps, the one in the north where the Marines are. Tough fighting. Now they are going to Vung Tau. In fact, they got on a flight before me, because they signed up at eight o'clock. About the war, they feel if things go as they have, it may take three to four years. But it depends more on international events. Also, one said that China must also be reckoned with. I also agree. But we both hope not on the battlefield.

We discussed living costs. They were amazed at what happened to my four-hundred-dollar pay when I lived in Kansas City, and we concluded that to live on an American level is as difficult as for them to live in VN on theirs.

Also, they—and I believe all that they said was said with candor—felt they owed us much thanks. They felt all their advisors were "number one," which endeared me more to them.

All my love,
PCP

CHAPTER 9

❧

The trip back from Taiwan was quick and uneventful. A chopper at Can Tho was heading to Sa Dec, and I was back, a world away, in a matter of hours.

I had most of the gifts except the BB gun. As my friend told me, the Taiwan government did not "encourage" the people to have any guns.

I walked up the hard dirt road, heading toward my hooch, waving a hello to several Vietnamese soldiers along the way, and saw Plato standing outside the administration building.

"Pritchard! Soon as you get settled, come see me," he called out to me. "How was the trip, anyway?" He seemed to throw that in as an afterthought.

"Great!" I yelled back. But now I wasn't so sure. My left-handed instinct said something was wrong.

I continued on to my hooch, dropped my gear, and went straight back to the administration building. Plato was behind his desk, and it looked to me like he was waiting more than working.

"Bad news, old buddy," he began. "I know you're still a little high from your trip. You gotta tell me about it sometime. I've heard some great stories about Taiwan. Never been there."

He paused and drew a deep breath.

"Anyway, Turnage is in charge around here, Paul. You sure didn't do yourself any favors with that guy."

I stiffened, remembering my field report.

Plato raised his hands, opening them in a broad shrug.

"Anyway, Paul, the bottom line is, he got you assigned to Operation Phoenix."

```
                            HEADQUARTERS
                UNITED STATES MILITARY ASSISTANCE COMMAND, VIETNAM
                          APO San Francisco  96222

SPECIAL ORDERS                                              4 December 1968
NUMBER     339                     EXTRACT

21.  TC 253.  Fol DY ASG/REL announced.  NTI.

PRITCHARD, PAUL C.  05537526              1LT MI USA 9300 USA ADGRU IV Corps
(WO8V-05-F) APO 96215 dy/w An Giang Prov (Ad Tm 69)

Dy asg:   Intel Off (PHOENIX), Hoa Tan Dist, Go Cong Prov, IV Corps, Ad Tm 92,
          APO 96359  F91A/18B-003 DMOS 9301

Dy rel fr: Inter Off, An Giang Intel Tm, An Giang Prov, IV Corps, Ad Tm 69
           F91C/03-005 DMOS 9316
Eff date:  VOCOMUSMACV cfm 18 Sep 68

FOR THE COMMANDER:

OFFICIAL:
                                       CHARLES A. CORCORAN
                                       Major General, USA
                                       Chief of Staff

J. F. JACOBSEN
CPT  USA
Asst AG

DISTRIBUTION:
5 - AG-AO
2 - Indiv conc 201
3 - Indiv conc Pay
5 - Indiv conc
2 - AG-EM
2 - SA USAAG IV CTZ
2 - CORDS PHOENIX
```

My Phoenix Orders

I had heard of Operation Phoenix. It was vague, though. I thought it was something for SEALs and Special Forces and CIA types. I could tell from Plato's tone that the assignment, whatever it was, wasn't good.

"What the hell does that mean, Plato?"

"It means you go out to Gò Công province with a district team and then run a bunch of mercenaries out of the place. And it means you head out in twenty-four hours."

"Plato! This is a joke! What the shit can I do about this?" I had never heard of Gò Công, but I could see it now on the map behind Plato's desk. It was south of Saigon on the edge of the massive Rung Sat swamp.

"No joke, Paul. Turnage can do this to you. And in all honesty, you're the best man for the job from here."

In the initial confusion of my return from the comforts of Taipei and now in disbelief, I could suddenly picture every word of my field report.

"Plato! This is fucking crazy! I'm off to some godforsaken place to get my ass shot—all because Turnage screwed up? Does that make sense? He screwed up! I just wrote the truth in that report."

"Paul, I know. Listen, this is my job. I'm supposed to dot all the i's and cross all the t's. Believe me, it's done. The bastard volunteered you for it."

Plato was as frustrated as I. We were both caught. It was a brief eternity as I looked across the desk at Plato.

"There is at least some good news in all this bullshit, buddy." Plato was watching my expression. "You got your silver bar."

"Fine, Plato. Just fine. Bastard gives me my grade and then sends me out to die. Where's Colonel Bough anyway?" I asked. If Bough was around, maybe there was a shred of sanity left in the compound.

"Saigon. With Westmoreland. They pulled him up there. Paul, get settled. Tomorrow, be at the morning briefing. Turnage will pin the silver on you. The chopper's coming for you after lunch."

I was hardly listening now. "Lunch?"

"Yes, the chopper's coming after lunch. Tomorrow. After the ceremony."

"Lunch. Great. The last meal, is that it?" I said facetiously.

"I guess you could say that."

I spent the rest of the afternoon packing, giving away a few things, and cooling down. The other officers who shared my hooch all seemed to know about it, and they all seemed to know that it was more a sentence than an assignment.

They came in and out during the afternoon, as did everybody on my "get-me" list. They all wished me good luck. Most seemed sincere. I didn't really care. This was over. Sa Dec was history. I tried to focus on Gò Công as a new assignment, but I hit the old logic bypass every time and ended in anger. *Next exit, despair,* I kidded myself, knowing that I didn't have time for it, only to get ready. Anger was my energy source.

Dinner was more of the same. There were a few questions about Taiwan, but it was clear the word was out. I ate without much companionship, eating out of routine, anger fulfilling my hunger, and thought that maybe it was best this way.

This was one more part of war, the process of separation. You would somehow get separated from things like safety, commitments, and even mental stability and life for some. The enemy was often your own side.

I walked around the compound on that last night in Sa Dec, pacing out the anger, knowing I was going to have to start all over, entertaining a few wild ideas, like calling my congressman, and then deciding that that was a joke.

The club was quiet, but at least there was a sense of quiet support from men who knew they could have been the one, from men who were learning from me not to cross Turnage. There were a few beers but no celebration. I was leaving, but it wasn't like I was rotating back to the States. Every man in the club knew that it was the worst assignment in the region.

There was one small favor. Charlie dropped no bombs on Sa Dec that night, and once asleep, I got a good night's rest. I ate breakfast and walked toward the headquarters building for the morning briefing. I saw Major LaRue. He was returning from an operation and joined me.

"Understand we're going to lose you, Paul," LaRue offered.

"Yes, sir. It was news to me when I returned."

"Well, it was news to me, too." He said it with some emphasis. We stopped for a moment outside the building and he continued. "Paul, Turnage is one of those commanding officers who values loyalty over judgment. I want you to know that you made the right judgment in your report. And you made the right decision when you told us about the problems with Turnage pushing his counterpart."

"Major…" I began, but he stopped me.

"He'll probably get me out of here next. I've got forty days left, so he'll have to work hard to get me sent up the river." It sounded like a challenge with a bitter edge. "But let's get back to you."

We started walking again.

"Turnage wants to pin the silver bar on you this morning. We've also got a Bronze Star for you that Colonel Bough approved before he left. You're a good soldier, Paul. I just wish to hell this hadn't happened. We could use you in the army. Don't let this prejudice you against a career, Paul."

LaRue was playing the father role. But I also read something else that I didn't like. The quiet message was that he thought I'd been shit on and wasn't sure I'd be tough enough to take it.

"Sir, I think this is a raw deal, if I understand the new assignment correctly," I said. "I did my job, and I did it right. And this is what it earned me. A career is pretty far from my mind right now. I just want to survive the next three months."

"Right." LaRue was back to being an officer now. "Well, I understand, Lieutenant."

We walked into the old building and up to the operations center, then to the rear of the building, back to the general's briefing room. Turnage was waiting at the back of the room for the general and his entourage, talking to the staff. He followed my entrance, still talking. The door to the general's office opened. The general walked directly to his front-row seat, and Turnage moved quickly to sit next to him. The staff of the two armies seated themselves.

"Good morning, gentlemen. Today is…" Captain Williams was on.

I said the lines in my head, just as I had said them out loud, up there in the front of the room on so many occasions. The wording and the protocol of the morning briefing were so familiar to me. The G2 report came and went, then the G3. My mind wandered.

Turnage was absolutely the wrong guy for this job, I thought. How he got into this slot was an amazement. Why didn't the Vietnamese complain? They certainly had the clout to object to an officer with Turnage's attitude toward the ARVN being assigned to this unit. Why didn't they? Maybe the general didn't like the major whom Turnage had chewed out. Or maybe the general just didn't want to raise a fuss. My thoughts bounced around my condition.

They were now into the discussions about future plans. It was the same briefing, the same talk every day. I looked around the room. There wasn't an officer in the room who was close to Turnage. Certainly none were looking forward to serving under his headship, if you could call it that. Maybe I was the lucky one.

"General, with your indulgence…" The briefing was over, and Turnage was on his feet. "We want to wish one of our young officers a farewell and best wishes in his new assignment."

The general was silent but signaled Turnage to continue.

"Lieutenant Pritchard! Front and center."

I rose from my chair. Here it was, my moment, and every eye in the room followed me, every ear activated for the slightest jab. I walked to the front of the briefing room and stood at attention in front of Turnage.

Turnage turned to the assembled men. "Lieutenant Pritchard here has been a real member of the team."

I was surprised for a moment. It sounded like praise, praise he didn't really have to offer at this point.

"Therefore," continued Turnage, "when Saigon asked for our best troops to help them out with an important new program, we had a fine officer to send."

Very nice. I knew Turnage would have had a hard time sending anyone else in the room. As a lieutenant, I was junior to most of the advisors. Anyway, no one wanted to go. There were few who volunteered in Vietnam. And even for those few, this would not have been one of the jobs on the list.

"Lieutenant Pritchard is also the recipient of his silver bar today. Actually, it's a few days early, but we got Saigon's approval to pin it on before he leaves."

Turnage did the honors.

"And we have a Bronze Star for your work here," Turnage continued. "Saigon doesn't usually give these away while you are still on assignment. You did a good job during Tet, Lieutenant." He placed the pin on my uniform and handed me a blue box. He didn't read the citation but handed it to me. "Well, Lieutenant, would you like to say anything?" Turnage offered.

In fact I did. I was ready, too, with a direct and frontal volley at Turnage, and I wanted to get it off my chest. Turnage was sending me to a place where people killed for the fun of it. I was ready to tell him that I knew why.

"Trung We…"

To the surprise of the entire room, the general rose and addressed me with my new rank. A higher order of silence fell on the room, greater than the normal quiet of the briefing. The general did not address a junior officer. Period.

"Trung We, you have done a fine job. We will miss you." The general spoke with perfect diction, firm, aloof. "But," he continued, "just as in my army, those in your army make the decisions. I do not have to agree with them. I doubt if you agree. Therefore, Trung We, we will recognize your contribution with our own Staff Honor Medal."

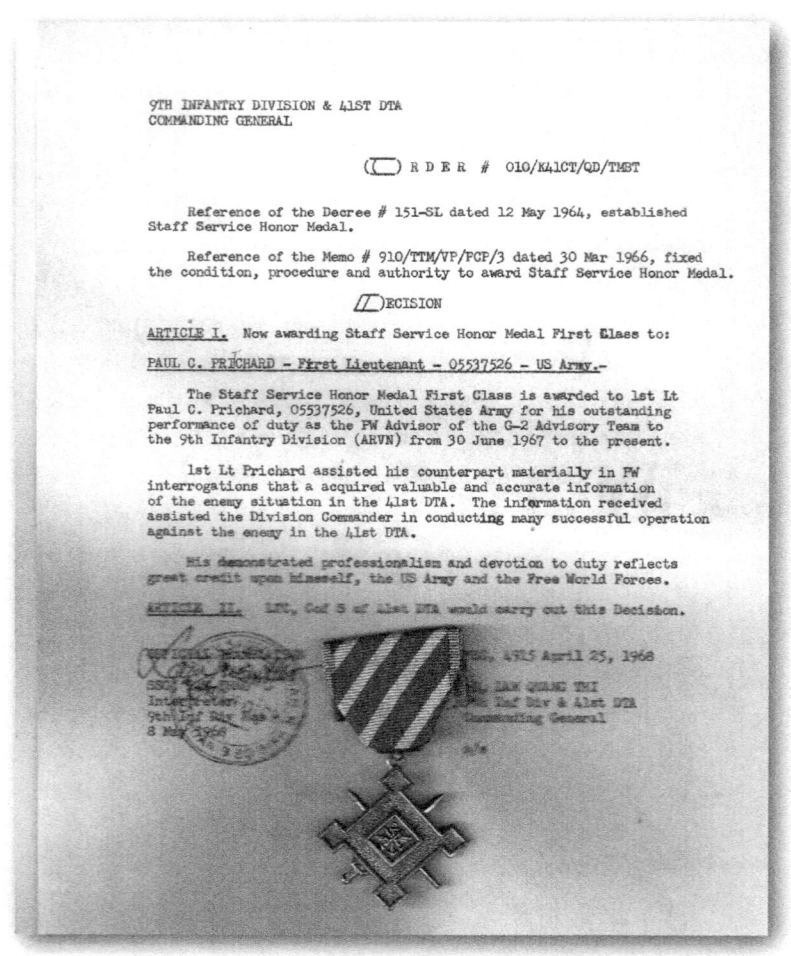

The Vietnamese Staff Service Honor Medal First Class

The general's staff was instantly on their feet, there before me with the pin. It was a gold pin with a green-and-red ribbon that reminded me of a Christmas decoration. The general pinned it on my uniform.

"We wish you success and good health, Trung We."

I stood at attention. The general, I thought, had said it all and perfectly. I saluted the general after responding to his proffered hand for a handshake.

"General," I said, looking straight at the general and without acknowledging Turnage. "It has been an honor to serve with your men. I have learned much from them. I have valued their friendship. I know I will remember your leadership and the lessons I have learned. Thank you for this medal and this honor. It is something I will never forget."

The general smiled.

An errant thought shot through my brain. Shit…I had completely forgotten about the BB gun. The man's son was probably still pestering him.

The general saluted me, and I walked to the rear of the room.

"Is there anything else, Colonel?" he asked Turnage.

"No, General."

The general turned to the seated men. "Thank you, gentlemen." He moved to the door. The silence from the unexpected still filled the room.

The men stood to leave, and Turnage walked out of the room. He walked by me without a glance. But as the rest departed, the officers shook my hand, offering their best hopes.

LaRue was last.

"I didn't want to tell you about the Vietnamese medal," he offered.

We walked out of the room in silence.

"You did a fine job in there."

I decided not to explain that the general may have kept me from attacking Turnage.

"Good luck, Major. I've enjoyed working with you."

Dear Mom and Dad,

I just got back from Taiwan. I hope you got my letters from there. Today was the day I got that silver bar pinned on my collar.

Let me tell you about a trip I made before I went to Taiwan. The G2 advisor, Major LaRue, was on R&R in Australia, so I filled in for him with the General, Colonel Turnage, the senior advisor, and Colonel Bate, the G3 advisor in charge of plans. (The only rank I had was that I was the senior second lieutenant, which is a rather insignificant honor. Even the general's first lieutenant outranked me.)

We flew down to Tra Vinh, the province headquarters for Vinh Binh province, to see how resupply and repairs were coming. We first rode around the town and saw the places the VC had held, including the house and headquarters of the province chief, Lieutenant Colonel Quah. The US Army MACV house was the only place not taken. Then we got back in the chopper and observed an operation from two thousand feet, actually watching the VC fighting back for the tree line. After a brief chase by some armored vehicles (called APC), they surrendered.

Then we flew over an area where we were resupplying outposts. Most were down to nothing because of the Tet offensive.

Lunch was the amazing thing. We flew back to Tra Vinh and were whisked through the town in the special VIP vehicle to the province chief's home (equivalent to a governor but a military man with many political connections).

There, we were seated in a large anteroom on massive white sofas. The general was in good humor, but I constantly reminded myself that he did not like people to stare or look too often at him. And he, himself, when he talks to someone, does not look at them when he addresses them.

We were given fragrant and refreshing hand towels to clear the dust from our faces and hands. Then Black & White scotch was poured with soda, which was savored with the general's conversation with the US and ARVN majors and colonels. The junior Americans were not spoken to except occasionally and then only to "clue us in" on why they had just laughed.

The general rose and went into the dining room, a large rectangular room with a long white table, our chairs, and an old Westminster clock on the wall that, by my watch, was fifteen minutes off. We were shown our seats by soldier-servants who put the general on one side, Colonel Bough next to him on his left, and the province chief across from him. I was seated last, of course, at the opposite side with the ARVN officers and on the left end facing the general. And well that was for, the less conspicuous, the better I felt.

The plates were very nice china with a flower pattern. Their bright-blue tint matched the blue of the walls, except for the occasional red pockmark where bullets must have struck the inside of the red clay building.

First, the headwaiters brought a plate with baked duck, green peas, and brown gravy. We each took a piece.

They had planned for the American guests, because all had a fork, a knife, and a spoon. Long sliced bread rolls were placed before us, and the Vietnamese first lieutenant across from me seemed to like only the doughy portion, as he broke off the rest, the crust, and surrounded his plate with the pieces. I had to watch myself, because his techniques with the fork and knife very obviously resembled those of one who wished he had a pair of chopsticks.

Colonel Hays and I have grown to be close friends. He had been to Taiwan, so during the periods of Vietnamese chatter, we would talk of the adventures of Taiwan. He was across from me, between the general and the first lieutenant. After we had finished our duck, all (except me) pulled out cigarettes. The funny thing was that the first lieutenant also pulled out a miniature pipe, screwed the cigarette he had down into the bowl, and then asked Colonel Hays for a light. Colonel Hays looked across at me with a big smile but was unable to conceal it when the first lieutenant sensed our surprise and looked at us. The Vietnamese lieutenant then proceeded to smile as if that were the only way to smoke a cigarette.

After the cigarettes, coffee (very strong) and tea (very weak) were served, two cups to each. Also, a plate of watermelon slices was placed before us with small forks. It was very good, even though I chewed up the seeds rather than duplicate the first lieutenant, who found it quite proper to spit them out on the tablecloth or on the floor, whichever suited him at the moment.

Coffee, then more cigarette smoke (and American cigarettes, too, even though they are black market), more Vietnamese sounds, like Bing Crosby "ba ba ba boo-ing" out a song, then the ceremonial rise with the general and all exiting after grateful thanks to the province chief. Then, whiz, back out to the airfield and more sightseeing.

One day, a long day, packed with unforgettable sights. Thought you'd like to hear about them. Keep warm, and keep those flowers blooming. See you in four.

P.

CHAPTER 10

⚜

THE WORST KIND OF TERROR, I decided, was the kind that came when you denied what you feared could happen, and then it happened. It was like walking into the same door twice, like dreaming some nightmare night after night.

I had been picked up in Sa Dec and flown to Can Tho, where I spent a night with some military intelligence friends. None of them knew much about Operation Phoenix. The administrative officer at Can Tho advised me that I'd get a full briefing when I arrived in Gò Công. "No sweat, man, you can handle it."

Roaring through the clouds toward my destination deep in the delta, I found myself focused on time. I had spent nine months at Sa Dec. I had just three months until I rotated back to the States. That was the goal: survival, home.

The chopper was to land at the Chu Ba district headquarters. I saw the blue flare, burning the message to the pilot that landing was secure. Shit. Nothing was "secure." Not this site, not this land, not me. I spotted four waiting GIs. They were lined up against the wall of a building that looked like a miniature castle, surrounded by a moat filled with concertina wire, radiating its concentric circles. The landing pad was so small that the Americans had to stay back at the castle. I tossed my duffel bag out and followed it.

The castle, it was clear to me, was the base, a safe haven. It was equally clear from the circular craters outside the moat that it had been under attack. I could see a dirt road to the west. Several Vietnamese were traveling along it toward some frail streamers of smoke visible to the north in a tree line. I strained my eyes. A village was remotely visible.

One of the Americans ran out to the chopper. He was dressed in a fatigue T-shirt and field pants. Extending his hand for a quick shake of mine, he grabbed my duffel bag and ran back. I adjusted the remaining load of M16, shoulder straps, and another duffel bag and followed him.

"Welcome, Lieutenant. I'm Major Ott. This is Private Wooten, Sergeant Bellamy, and Lieutenant English. Let's get you settled in our temporary home. We're running an operation out of here."

I followed him into the bunker. It was a dark room, lit with a single bulb and the sunlight from the open door. The room was about twenty by forty feet with four beds around the sides of one end, a table in the middle, and a kitchen area at the other end.

"This is your bunk, Lieutenant." Major Ott pointed.

The bunk was obviously mine. The other three were well-identified territory with clothes on wall hooks, an occasional family picture, and several *Playboy* posters on the wall. I tossed my gear on the bunk as Ott continued.

"Lieutenant, I'm glad to have somebody with some experience with us. We understand you know this war pretty well."

"Thank you, sir," I replied. The room was cooler than the sun-fried outdoors but not cool enough. It had a stillness that kept the sweat running. Everyone but Ott had stripped down to T-shirts, and I did the same.

"How long have you been in country?" It was English, now seating himself at the table. The men moved around the room, settling themselves here and there, but were quiet. They were all listening to us.

"Nine months. Mostly with the Ninth ARVN. I was a recon company advisor and interrogation officer." I joined English and Ott at the table. "What's the situation here?" I asked.

"Lieutenant," Ott began, "we've got an operation tonight. I'm going with you."

He said it firmly, leading me to two possible conclusions. Either he wanted to check me out, or he hadn't seen much action himself and wanted to be part of the operation.

"What's the operation?"

"I just got briefed on it this morning at province headquarters," Ott replied. "The OSA chief has a report that one of the VC leaders is back in his village with his family now, in U Dau over in the next district." He paused, resting his elbows on the edge of the table. "Sorry you have to hit the ground running, but this guy is somebody they want, and the war waits for none of us."

Ott's bit of philosophy seemed out of place. It was the kind of add-on that led me to believe it pertained to his own situation more than mine.

"What time do we head out?" I asked.

"Midnight," Ott replied. "Sergeant Bellamy will go with us. English," he said, looking across the table at the officer, "you and Wooten will stay here."

"Who do we have working with us?" I asked.

"You have a squad, Lieutenant," Ott replied quickly, looking at me, in a tone that suggested that I should have known. "You'll meet them at dinner."

I was a little puzzled.

"Major, who are they? Do we know anything about them?"

"Your predecessor handpicked them," Ott offered as though that would answer the question. It didn't, and it raised another one.

"Major, what happened to him, my predecessor?" I asked, realizing that I had overlooked a critical issue here. "Who was he?"

"He was First Lieutenant Jerry Becker. He volunteered for the Phoenix operation. Unfortunately, he had only seen duty in Saigon. They took him out when I arrived here last week."

I sat back in the chair with a silent sigh. I watched Ott watching me, waiting for the next question. So Ott was new. Brand new, by the look of him. Even his fatigues were new. He was new to this assignment and probably new in country. No wonder the other men were so quiet. His armor insignia confirmed that he was a duck out of water, an officer trained to use tanks but instead was assigned to an infantry war.

"What happened to him?" I asked, knowing already.

"He took a round in the stomach trying to get his squad to move on a machine gun." It was English who replied.

The John Wayne image had just taken another American in Vietnam. I didn't want to know if Becker had lived. It didn't really matter at the moment. It was all luck and skill, 90 percent the former, 10 percent the latter.

There was noise outside the door, sounds of human movement. One of the popular force troops called out a greeting. Private Wooten poked his head out the door.

"The squad," he announced, glancing at Ott. "They are coming in, sir."

"We'll meet them outside."

"Tell Le Be we'll be out in a minute." Ott now rose from the table. "Come on, Lieutenant, let's meet your men."

I followed Ott. There were three men outside, waiting for us. They came in varying sizes but were large Asian men, obviously of mixed nationality. The largest looked to be a Cambodian. He stepped forward quickly as we emerged and offered me his hand.

"Bonjour, Lieutenant."

"Bonjour," I replied to his apparent pleasure.

His face broke into a large smile as he shook my hand.

"Lieutenant, this is Bodai. He's their leader," Ott said. "Can you speak French?"

I nodded and worked my way through the niceties of French introductions. I wanted to know these men and their names. Bodai's French was hard to catch at first. It was heavily accented with something else, probably his native Cambodian.

They caught sight of movement in the distance, and I looked down toward the road. There were four men walking up the narrow path from the road. Bodai followed my eyes and shouted out to the men. They made the rest of the distance at a full run. Bodai introduced each of them, all men of mixed Chinese, Vietnamese, and Cambodian heritage, it seemed. But all of them in pretty good shape. None were winded after their run.

Ott had stood off to the side as Bodai and I went through the introductions. Then he and Wooten moved back toward us.

"Wooten, where the hell is the interpreter?" he asked.

Bodai must have caught his tone and assumed his question, because he replied to me in French, "I think he is still in town."

Ott seemed to understand even before I could translate.

"Shit, that guy is undependable! Where do we get these interpreters, anyway?" Ott mused. He shook his head in frustration. "Well, at least, you can communicate with Bodai."

Ott turned to go back to the bunker, and I could now see more movement, a few more men, but these were in uniform. They were making their way toward the little castle. I gave Bodai a quizzical look, and he saw the men.

"Popular front," Ott explained. We started walking back to the bunker. He sighed. "VC mortar fired us two nights ago. We do not know if the VC are trying to keep us busy so we do not go on operations, or if the VC plan to attack us."

Bodai and his men headed for their small metal shelter.

When we reentered the bunker, Sergeant Bellamy was on the radio, apparently finishing his communications. He was concentrating on some written notices in front of him, translating the message. Ott waited by his side as he worked between his code book and the paper.

"Looks like the operation is a go, sir."

Ott nodded.

"We'll be picked up by province troops at 2300 hours, sir. SEAL will be in support on the PBRs. If they get to the village first, they'll signal us that they're going in. We cut off access from our side."

Bellamy stopped for a moment, checking his code book again. "Code name for the PBRs is 'Blue Boy.' SEAL team is 'Wild Buck.' Sir,"—Bellamy grinned up at Ott—"seems like somebody knew what they were talking about."

Ott almost smiled back but didn't. He turned to me.

"It's crazy Markowski leading the SEAL team. The village will be lucky if any of them make it alive. Sit down, Lieutenant. Let's go over this thing."

Ott and I sat at the table. He spread a map across its surface and pulled some notes from his pocket.

"To the north of us," he began, his fingers on the map, "right here, is the Rung Sat. I don't know how much you know about our situation. Saigon figures that most of the VC getting into the capital district are operating out of this swamp. But here, all around here, are villages. Their families are all in these villages around the swamp."

Ott pulled his chair in closer, still looking at the map.

"One of their leaders is a North Vietnamese. Saigon thinks he's the big boss. We're going to get him tonight when he visits his family. The SEAL Markowski will come in from the river here. We'll walk in on the rice dike there. You, me, and your Phoenix team."

I tried to find Ott's eyes, which were still on the map. I tried to sense how Ott felt about headquarters' accuracy, about murdering a man while he relaxed with his family. Ott knew I was probing. He kept his eyes on the map. The silence was filled with my question. But I was not conveying judgment, only seeking the conviction and morality of my superior.

I couldn't tell if Ott liked this plan. I certainly did not. But Ott was a career armor officer who was trying to make the best of it. I had learned long ago that, if you're career and you want to get ahead, you have to show that you can make it in other branches. If you're armor, you do your time in artillery or infantry. Infantry, of course, was the big test. I guessed that was why Ott was here.

My eyes were on the map, too, trying at some level to memorize it, knowing how vital it was, realizing how little it really said.

"Major, I've got to tell you…" I began with some uncertainty.

Ott looked up at me for the first time in several minutes.

"Major, I haven't even had a briefing on the local situation, but we're going to be exposed on that dike on three sides."

Ott cut me off.

"Lieutenant, before I left Saigon last week, I was told that you're good. You made it nine months in Sa Dec, and you've got excellent ratings. We'll be OK. Anyway, it's the province's plan. That's all."

"Last week?" My mind reeled. Last week! Last week, I was in Taipei. Ott knew last week that I was coming. That meant Turnage had marked me even before Colonel Bough had left Sa Dec. The irony was bitter and the picture in my mind bleak. There I was in Taipei; Turnage was in Sa Dec, signing my papers.

"Lieutenant." Ott got up, his eyes now focused on me. "The army doesn't wait for you or anyone else. This guy is coming back to his village tonight."

For the next hour or so, I settled in physically, while my mind added up the score. This was a joke. And one terrible set of odds. I didn't know my men. I didn't know the terrain. I didn't know the local enemy tactics. I had the uncomfortable feeling that these VC were pros, not like the ones around Sa Dec.

I went outside and smoked a cigarette with Bodai. We talked of his home in Cambodia.

"Two sons," he bragged.

Wooten broke the silence. "Major! Convoy's coming!" he yelled in the door.

It was good timing for both Ott and me. We had been separated. I was still pissed about this mission. I had the feeling that Ott understood that. But neither of us had a choice. It was best to get going. I would just go with the flow. A sort of fatalism seemed to govern my reactions.

I went in and grabbed my M16, eyeglass strap, and shoulder pack. I adjusted the web belt that held my canteen, first aid kit, and cartridge clips. I checked the taping on the clips. I had learned long ago at Sa Dec from Litzenger how to tape two clips together in reversed positions, a process that he called "sixty-nine-ing." It wasn't standard procedure, and it could cause the weapon to malfunction, but it worked. It kept more ammunition where you needed it, and at least, so far, I hadn't seen any malfunction of the feeding mechanism.

The convoy, if you could call it that, was three old ARVN deuces and two jeeps. My squad was already mounting up when Ott, Bellamy, and I walked down the path that led from the castle bunker to the road. Ott pointed to the first jeep. I knew I had to pay my respects to Ott's Vietnamese counterpart, who was waiting in the front seat. Ott introduced us briefly, and the Vietnamese major nodded. Ott jumped in the back seat, and I joined him.

Dumb shit, I thought. Two of us here. But I wasn't going to question Ott in front of his counterpart.

The convoy moved northwest. I watched everything. The dark was deepening, making my task of creating a mental map more difficult. I watched every direction, every civilian grass hut we passed, trying to memorize the locations of unique features along the road. The paddies were glistening smooth with the river water that had filled the fields forever. The dikes were dark brown, also glistening with moisture. There was an occasional water buffalo resting, his day of pulling a plow now over. I strained to find the tree lines.

The number of roadside huts increased as we approached the outskirts of a province town. The road turned from dirt hardened by centuries of use into some kind of pavement. Soon I could see thatch-roofed huts, shops, and then plaster buildings like those in Sa Dec. The convoy pulled into a walled area that was crowded with military vehicles, guards, and old buildings and houses.

"Let's go meet the SEAL," Ott said as we jumped out of the jeep. I followed him toward one of the buildings: a residential structure of worn grandeur, a firm reminder of the French colonial days. The Vietnamese major drove off in the jeep, heading toward another building. Ott seemed unconcerned.

We walked up a set of broad, low steps to a tile veranda, then across it and into the dark of a generous hallway. We paused for a moment, and a door opened. An American emerged: a civilian dressed in khaki trousers, sandals, and a white shirt with its tail out.

"You eaten, Major?" he asked abruptly.

"No, we just had enough time to get the lieutenant here in," Ott responded.

"Welcome, Lieutenant. I'm your control."

"Sir?" I had had enough cryptic messages today.

"Sorry, buddy. Guess I should introduce myself. I'm Peter Lister. I'm with OSA, and I'm in charge of the Phoenix operation here." He shook my hand, then pointed to another door. "Let's eat."

We followed him into a large dining room, and the three of us sat down at a table set for four.

"Dwain's sleeping. Maybe he'll join us. He likes to rest before operations," Lister offered in explanation of the vacant place at the table.

We were served by a single Vietnamese man. Dinner was French bread, rice, clams, and tea. We ate for a few moments in relative silence. Lister got up and walked over to a low cupboard that filled one wall of the dining room. Extracting a bottle of scotch, he returned to the table.

"This will help it," he said, pouring the scotch into his glass of tea.

Ott and I waved off his offer for us to do the same.

Lister ate quickly for a few more minutes and then began talking as rapidly as he had eaten. He had a manner that I always associated with people from New England.

"Here's the situation. We've got a big one tonight. And I want him. Dwain will go in by PBR. You and Ott will be backed up by the ARVN. Pritchard, you and your men will be responsible for controlling the main path into the village. It's an easy job. Just don't step on a mine."

Ott was silent, still eating.

"Lister, how many men is this guy going to have with him?" I asked.

"No idea, Pritchard. We've never been this close to him."

I chewed on that one with my clams for a moment. The odds were stacking up in my head.

"I'm gonna get Dwain up," Lister said as he rose from his seat.

"Wait one," I blurted out. I couldn't figure out the relationship of the civilian to Ott. It seemed like Ott was suddenly a symbol of the US Army in Vietnam: not in control, doing what it was told by the State Department. And the State Department was run by "hypers."

Lister paused. The brevity of this mission briefing amazed me.

"Mr. Lister, if we are supposed to capture or kill some guy, I would like to know a little more about him. I mean, I don't even know what he looks like! Am I supposed to assume that every adult male Vietnamese I see is this guy?"

"Pritchard, you catch on quick," Lister responded. "Anyway, if this guy is as good as we think he is, you may not have time to do anything more than cut loose with whatever fire power you've got."

He moved toward the door. Ott and I rose, too, pushed our chairs in, and followed him back into the darkness of the hallway. Ott still said nothing.

"Listen, Pritchard," Lister said as he led us down the hallway. "You've been out there where they hit and run. The guys you've been dealing with are classic guerrillas. This guy and his men are pros. They fight guerrilla. They fight conventional. The only thing we've got going for ourselves tonight is surprise."

Surprise! Bullshit, I thought, looking at Lister. I knew that it was important. But I tried to find the other element, the original patience. I could see no patience whatsoever in Lister. I recalculated the odds in my head like a one-arm slot machine recalculating the potential payoff every time another quarter was fed into the machine. Two conclusions kept coming up. Patience was the key. I doubted we had a surprise here anyway.

We entered what seemed to be a bedroom with no windows, dark and large. I could make out the outlines of a sizeable bed covered with a mosquito net, an end table, and one low lamp lighting a table surface. There wasn't much else in all that space.

Dwain was already up. He wore black Vietnamese pants and was putting on a shirt when we walked in. He was never going to hide behind the indigenous clothes. He was well over six feet and built like a frog, I thought, with a huge torso supported by an unlikely set of slender, tapered legs.

"You the fresh meat?" he asked, not bothering to stop what he was doing.

"Lieutenant Pritchard has been in country for enough time. He's got a good record. He's seen plenty of action." It was Ott who replied to Dwain.

"Terrific. Another hero, huh?"

"No. I just want to survive this thing," I countered.

Inexperienced as he was, Ott seemed to understand that there were more than personalities in conflict here. He cut off any exchange between us.

"Lister, we're going to go over our plans. I'm the new guy out tonight, and I want to make sure I make it back safe and sound," Ott said calmly.

Dwain was silent. I was growing more impressed with Ott.

Lister, Ott, and I gathered at the table in the dark room, where Lister laid out an unfolded map. Lister looked at both of us and said quietly, "Don't mind Dwain. He always gets uptight before an operation."

Dwain joined us at the table, his shirt open and a pistol in the holster under his armpit.

"Dwain, we'll give Ott and Pritchard time to get to this schoolhouse," Lister began rapidly, tracing the movement on the map, tapping it with his fingers for emphasis. "You're on the PBR and heading away from the village so that, if anyone is wondering what's going on, they won't see you heading for this place. It's going to be pitch black out there with no moon. So you have your PBR cut across the river, move up on the other side, and then pass the village. Then you cut back across and down to this point where this canal comes in. You and your men get on shore and follow the river path into the village."

I listened to Lister's plan. He sounded like a coach, hyped up by the game, reminding his quarterback that plays were going to be called from the sideline.

Lister went over the layout of the village and the probable location of guards. He noted with certainty the locations of motorized boats that the PBR crew would monitor in case the VC tried to use them. I wondered how accurate his information was.

"Pritchard, there is only one trail out to the road." Lister pulled me from the concentration of trying to memorize the map. "That means that they may cut across the rice paddy if they want to escape that way. You take your men and close off that trail. You'll have about an hour to wait, here, at this schoolhouse. Then you start moving. Try to get as close to the village as you can. Dwain will be getting out of the PBR at 0300. It shouldn't take him more than twenty minutes to make it down the river trail to the village."

"What happens if we take fire, Lister?" I asked.

"Well, that shouldn't happen, since 'our boy' will either go for the boats to get across the river to the Rung Sat, at which point the PBR will pick them up, or he'll take the trail that Dwain is coming down."

"There's another possibility, and he just might take it, since they will have some idea of the size of my squad. What happens if he comes our way?" I asked.

Dwain grinned at me. "Then the army will have to do the job."

He was right, of course, but that was no easy comfort for me on a first operation with a new squad facing some of the best North Vietnamese.

Ott and I walked back to join Bellamy by the waiting vehicles, and everyone loaded up except Ott's counterpart. The convoy seemed to know where to go.

About an hour later, we arrived at the schoolhouse as planned. An interpreter explained to the ARVN that they were to guard the school grounds down to the place where the path split. Then they would wait there. The ARVN troops seemed to already know the plan.

Ott, Bellamy, and I entered the schoolhouse, and Ott immediately sank to the floor, his back against the wall.

"Let's get some sleep," he suggested.

It was inviting, sleep. I was dead tired, pushing eighteen hours. But I was too charged up to sleep. The night was black, humid, and still. My clothes were drenched with sweat. I watched the squad as they rested, smoked cigarettes in the dark, tried to relax. I thought about Dwain and wondered about the differences between us. Maybe there weren't too many after all. I suspect that both of us succeeded because we wanted to survive, whether or not we wanted to be heroes.

The signal came to go. I woke Ott. We walked out the door and followed the ARVN, who were already heading down the road. We had walked only a short distance when I stopped short. In the silence that we all sought, I heard a sound, a metal rattle from Ott's direction, just the sort of thing that identified the inexperienced and offered us up for easy ambush.

"Major," I said, stopping him. "What's that noise?"

"I knew I shouldn't have brought it," Ott replied quietly, smiling. He reached into his side pocket and pulled out a cottage cheese tub. "Just some M&Ms. Here, help me finish them off." He poured a bunch into my hand. "My wife sends them over."

I had to smile at him. There was finally some humor, though very little, in this horrendous day. Here we were, I thought, on a well-planned and expensive operation, numerous lives at risk, and the major had brought along M&Ms in an empty cottage cheese container.

We walked on, refocusing on the thought of mines, stepping carefully. It sounds simple, but I found it very hard to step in exactly the same spot as the mercenary in front of me. When we came to the junction of the road and the trail, the ARVN troops spread out, leaving my squad to walk on.

Without a word, the squad continued down the path. It was narrow, dark, and very wet. It was not good. Ott was behind me when I heard a mechanical click and saw light for a second. I stopped and swung around in the same movement. Everyone else dropped, poised, waiting.

Ott had calmly pulled out a penlight and flashed it on for an instant. "We're...we're...on time," he stammered, now aware of the effect.

"Major, please don't use that again," I said, doubting that he needed to be told.

In a few more steps, there was another screwup. This time it was a splash. One member of the squad had slipped off the side of the path and into the water. Wondering how the hell we were going to survive with all of these mistakes and afraid to think about what they were doing to my odds, I motioned the men to stop and take off their boots. At least we would have more traction in bare feet.

We all sat down to get out of our boots. As we sat, we all heard the movement, coming from behind us. We readied. It was the interpreter and two ARVN men coming from the road.

"VC gone," the interpreter said simply. "We go." The sense of relief was clear.

Whatever had happened to cause the cancellation, it was just fine with me. As we walked back to the schoolhouse, I mentally counted up the number of times I had been out on a mission and felt this kind of incredible relief when it was aborted. It always felt great, but there were too many of those times, I thought, too many to be winning a war.

We made it back to the province town and slept in the advisory team compound.

"Temporary home," Ott called it. "We got a few days to rest. Get to know the town," he suggested.

But I knew it was time to write home. Time to face the challenge of truth. Somehow, though, I didn't know the truth yet about my situation. But I felt I was coming to some better understanding of the truth of this war.

Dear Mom and Dad,

I've been at Gò Công province for the last two days. Mom, look on your map south of Saigon. We are north of the city that I described where we came and had dinner with the general and the province chief.

There's more I can tell you about the town. It's plush. Tall, solitary, aspiring trees provide enough shade to keep it pleasant, cooled by the ocean located just on the edge of the province.

I've caught up on some needed rest and done some serious thinking about this very serious war. Much of what we have seen built, or were told was built, has crumbled in a matter of days. Charlie, although he has been drawn out of the places he has secretly occupied, has demonstrated that he can pick the date and the place to thwart anything we have done.

One of the basic problems that we have discovered is that we are so dependent on the VN for information—from all of our intelligence to how many VC are captured after an operation. So much misinformation had occurred that we were misled, deceived. Thus we were off guard when everything occurred. We have been so preoccupied with being fair and not pushing these people. We try to ward off any criticism of neocolonialism, so afraid to demand results in satisfying the legitimate needs of the paddy people that we have accepted the half-truths too often.

Despite my antipathy for the French, they did recognize that this government is incapable of ruling their own with any sort of justice or effort to bring about justice. Of course, the French did little to educate the masses but just subjugated them.

Coupled with this is the nature of the people. Looking far back in their history, there is the ever-present story of the military hero, most of whom were warlords. Today, the generals are continuing that history. Power rests in the hands of the military leaders as evidenced by the president and the vice president. They maintain defensive postures because they risk nothing and recover tribute from those they protect. If they try to win an offensive victory, they lose troops, and troops are the basis for their power, the amount of power they can march in Saigon either to support or fight another warlord. We have walked into an awesome thing left with little choice. They threaten our influence in Asia. We have to protect the political and thus the military leaders of Thailand, Singapore, Laos, Indonesia, Japan, Taiwan, the Philippines, New Zealand, and the Australian island continent.

We chose Vietnam as our stand. If we lose it, we cut off Laos, which then faces a Communist Vietnam, neutralist Cambodia, and Socialist Burma, let alone China. Thailand is then bordered by Communists, then Singapore, etc. Some people call it the domino theory and dispute the neo-isolationist theorists. It makes sense on paper. But it ignores history.

The isolation of America has been the cause of defect so far. We have tried to support these people in their war, let them fight it, etc., when we should have seen what they would do by a simple look at their history. War is a way of life here. Peace is a quality of mind, not of the state. Justice is guaranteed only by the most powerful. That is the set of truisms of Asia. And by the power cloaked in the black pajamas of communism or the white scarf of democracy, really it's just the same history repeating itself.

Solution? Solution one is to withdraw unconditionally. Result: (a) lose face (very destructive for a nation such as ours, since our economic and international power is based on military might) or (b) lose allies.

Solution two: fight the same. Result: ultimate need to withdraw, hopefully without defeat.

Solution three: take over the war effort or else demand greater control (not necessarily commitment, though) of the effort. Result: (a) if accepted by the VNs, then there's a good chance for victory but an outlook for the same type of situation as in Korea, Japan, Western Europe, Taiwan, i.e., the long-term establishment of a militarily imposed economic stability and political equilibrium; or (b) if the VNs refuse our demands, then withdrawal is justified (in the eyes of others and ourselves). Of course, it would mean renewed commitment in Thailand.

So goes the war. All is fairly quiet in the delta. Saigon seems to be the target now.

One last thing: see you in 124.

CHAPTER 11

❧

MAKING WAR CAN'T BE A democratic institution, I thought as I sat with Lister and Ott. Lister finished his brief explanation of the terminated operation.

"Dwain found the whole fucking village was empty. Hey, there'll be another chance! The VC chief must have known about the operation before we got there."

"Mr. Lister, we're lucky that their informer didn't give them more time to plan an ambush for us," I said.

Lister ignored me. He had been embarrassed by the failure. And he knew we knew he was a failure.

"Let me tell you how much I'm worried about you making contact," he snarled. He circled his index finger to the base of his thumb, making a little hole. "You see this, Lieutenant? This is the size of a rat's ass. That's how much I care. Anyway, I've decided to take your squad and deploy them with Dwain and the PBRs. We're gonna move into the Rung Sat faster when the SLAR pilots spot some movement. We haven't been too successful hitting them here in the province. So, Major, you guys might want to take some R&R, since we're going to be keeping Charlie pretty busy across the river."

"I appreciate that, Lister," said Ott. "We've got some other work in the district. It will be nice to know you're keeping Charlie occupied."

Ott rose from his chair, and I did the same. We walked out.

"Bastard!" Ott muttered as we crossed the veranda and headed down the steps. "If he knew there was a chance that the mission could have been compromised, he should have warned us."

I felt the same way. But I had lost my outrage at that kind of thing long ago when I learned that surprise had to be expected as the norm, not the exception. Nothing was ever done in secret in Vietnam when the ARVN were involved. It was hard enough to keep secrets in one army, let alone in two. And not to mention when we were partners with the ARVN.

"Major, we were damned lucky to get back without losing someone. And Lister…Lister seemed disappointed that no one got blown away by a mine or something."

"Bastard." Ott said it again, with even more conviction this time.

"I guess he thought it would have looked good to be able to report something to Saigon," I said.

"Yeah," Ott said at last, "I guess you're right. We're lucky that all we lost were my M&Ms."

I snorted a laugh in agreement.

Ott lapsed back into thought. We walked on in silence. He slowed and then stopped.

"Paul," he said, turning to me, "I don't understand how we are supposed to be fighting this war with these State Department guys always calling the shots. Were they in control of your other advisory team?"

I thought about the quiet control that the State Department guys at Sa Dec had exuded. They came and they went, ostensibly to monitor the war, I had thought then. "Major, I knew they were there, but that's all. I don't know if they were in command like they are with Phoenix. It was a big team."

"Well, I'm certainly glad they don't control the rest of my responsibilities like they do your program."

Ott fell silent again, but he picked up the pace of our walk. And when he broke the silence, it was in an almost cheerful tone of someone back in control on familiar territory.

"You know, Paul, I want to do something for our team. I want Sergeant Bellamy to get some R&R. And I want to get us a stove and refrigerator. You've been around. Can we get it done?"

"I think so, Major," I replied. "I know a fellow in Saigon who might be able to help us. But we'll need some Chicom rifles, sir. Have we got any?"

"Chicoms? Well, yes. About five, I think. Yeah, there were five last time I counted. What do we do with them?"

"We have to get them to Tan Son Nhut to the air force supply depot. It might take a day or two, but five Chicoms should do it. This guy trades them for other things, and every air force soldier going home has to have one as a souvenir."

Ott grinned in understanding. "What do you say we drive?"

I knew this was as much an invitation as a statement of command. But it was definitely not a question. I knew Ott was ticked off, and I had a pretty good idea about why. Blown operations time and again were bad enough. Lister was the salt. Whatever he did and however well he did it, he managed to treat both of us and our men like pawns in a cheap game of penny poker.

"I'll need to clear our trip to Saigon with the colonel," Ott mused, stopping short. "I'll meet you here," he said, already walking back across the vehicle parking lot toward the main headquarters building.

I waited for a few minutes by the jeep, then decided to take a walk down to the river and the dock. The deep roar of a navy patrol boat dominated the other sounds of the compound as I walked slowly along the river's edge. Take away that sound, and it would have been a timeless sort of scene: palm trees, local people in traditional garb going about their business, the quiet waters of a river delta, sampans moving slowly.

The PBR grew less distracting, more distant from the peaceful sight in front of me. I watched it as it moved a short way upstream to the bend in the river where a canal entered. A sampan was moving into the river from the canal. I could see the man under the coolie hat who guided it with a long shaft. He seemed to be talking, pointing, and explaining something to his two young ones, who watched the world from under a grass roof on the sampan's deck. I could see their mother, too. She was on the other side of the sampan, busy. I followed the family for a moment, then gazed down the river, taking in the pastoral setting.

Suddenly the PBR noise was a high whine. I looked back. It seemed to be circling in the water, and the crew were rushing to one side, leaning over.

Then the large gray boat stood still in the water, bobbing in its own wake like a toy at the beach.

Then I saw the bottom of the sampan in the water.

The wake of the PBR had capsized the sampan. The crew was trying to rescue the four passengers, the family I had been watching. The crew hustled back and forth across the deck of the big boat as the river suddenly became a congregation point for other sampans, rowboats, and anything that could get out on the water.

I was fixated on this action, straining my eyes. I watched the PBR crew pull people onto the boat. The few minutes seemed like an eternity. Then the smaller boats began to move off, and the PBR's engines surged. The big boat headed back in my direction toward the dock. As it arrived, I could see only two figures wrapped in the green-gray blankets. They were two adults. I looked back. The sampan was gone, and with it were the two children.

"What's happening?" It was Ott, who joined me.

"Our PBR just capsized a sampan. There were two kids on board. It looks like they're gone."

Ott's eyes followed the PBR's course toward the dock.

"Come on," he said, "let's find out what happened. See if there's anything we can do."

The dock was a beehive of activity, all centered around the mother, who swayed under her navy-issue blanket, issuing a high, whining, hysterical sound. Vietnamese, ARVN, navy crew, and people from the town swarmed around. As we approached, the navy interpreter was trying to translate her moaning sounds to the navy crew chief.

"Can we help, Chief?" Ott offered.

"No, sir. We can handle it." The navy chief turned and shouted to one of his crew, "Get me the book! Get me the damn book! How much do you pay them?"

Ott and I watched, a few steps removed from the growing crowd.

"Ask them if they are hurt," ordered the navy chief.

The translator spoke and then listened.

"No, sir. They both seem OK. The mother wants to know about her children."

"Tell her that the United States Navy is deeply saddened by the loss of her children."

The interpreter did his job. The effect was only to increase the level of the moaning, now at a higher pitch.

"Tell her that we wish to express our sorrow with a payment!" The navy chief had to shout over the din. The interpreter spoke, and his words seemed to have a quieting effect on both the parents and the crowd around them.

"Tell her we will pay two thousand piastres as an expression of our sympathy."

The interpreter started talking before the navy chief had finished. As he spoke, the mother's sobs stopped. The father now seemed animated, approaching the interpreter with interrogatives, it seemed.

"The father wants to know when you will pay this money."

Ott grabbed my arm.

"Let's get the fuck out of here. I don't need this."

The problem had been resolved, it seemed. The debt had been paid. The value of those kids' lives and their home was a few hundred dollars, enough to quiet the sobbing mother and the grieving father.

"Major, one thing I've learned over here is that life isn't worth much in war. Theirs or ours."

I wasn't sure how to explain it. Lister put lives at risk and loved it. I had just seen enough for a kind of stoic resignation about the real victims of war: children who wanted to discover, adults who yearned a simple life with their family, and naïve men who were part children when they went to war.

We mounted the jeep for the ride back to the castle bunker. The trip was filled only with the silence of disbelief and the quiet crumbling of values.

CHAPTER 12

❧

ACTUALLY, WE ALREADY HAD A stove. It just didn't work very well. But what the hell, we decided. If we were going after a refrigerator that ran on propane, why not try for a new stove as well?

Anyway, this was a mad lark, because it would require Ott and me to risk our lives during a long drive to find some appliances that might or might not be available. You could not, after all, just get on the telephone, call Saigon, and say, "Let me speak to Sergeant Winslow—you know, the guy who will scrounge some appliances for a few old Communist Chicom rifles that every GI wants to take home as a war trophy." No, you had to show up, find him, show him the rifles, hope he knew where the appliances were, load them onto your trailer, and drive back.

Or you could make a requisition and wait six months.

I must admit, though, the trip was exactly what I wanted to do. I felt much as I did when my brother and I "borrowed" Dad's car one weekend when they were away. Neither one of us was old enough to drive, but drive we did. We took a wild ride down to the local high school drive-in, made a few cruising rounds, and pulled in for a burger and an ice cream frosty. That scheme was completely unpremeditated, completely nonessential, and given our skills behind the wheel, completely risky.

This trip was the same kind of release and a welcome diversion from the containments of reality. I couldn't wait to get going.

It took two days to plan the trip. My squad had left. They went off without a comment or a protest after Ott and I saw Lister. I was sorry to see Bodai go. I liked him, and I knew we were losing invaluable knowledge when he headed down the road with his men. I had thought that he might be a little sorry, too, but not so. They were mercenaries, paid by the operation with a bonus for success. They seemed to measure life and honor and every other value on a different scale. Not worse or better than mine, I decided, just different.

"Sure you don't need someone to drive?" Private Wooten asked hopefully.

He was hitching the trailer to the jeep with Sergeant Bellamy giving an occasional guiding hand. I looked at Wooten, a nice kid, a little brother.

"You ever been to Saigon, Wooten?" I asked.

"Just when they shipped me in, sir. I was down here pretty quick."

"Let me ask the major."

I walked back to the bunker where Ott was packing.

"Major, what do you think about taking Wooten with us?"

Ott's response was immediate.

"Unless you think we will encounter some action, I think the two of us can handle it."

I walked back out to a very hopeful Wooten. "Sorry. You're needed here, Private." The private's face fell.

"Bellamy, Wooten, what can we bring you guys from Saigon?" I tried to be upbeat as they were checking out the jeep and its trailer.

"Well, sir, if you see any of those coin collectors selling Chinese coins on the street, buy me a couple of sets for my boys," Sergeant Bellamy replied.

I was pleasantly surprised. Here was a father thinking about his sons. Some values persisted. "Anything else, Sergeant?" I asked.

"Well…yes, sir. I guess so. If they have any big bags of M&Ms, well…the major and I both like them."

I laughed, remembering the first M&M operation.

"You got it, Sarge. Anything for you, Private?"

"Yes, sir, a one-way ticket home."

The honesty of Private Wooten's answer threw us back to the reality of where we were.

Then, realizing what he had done, Wooten quickly added, "Don't get me wrong, sir. I like the team. I just hope my tour gets over fast. But, if you can, get a case or two of Miller beer. I love it."

"If nothing else, Private, we'll bring back the beer."

Ott emerged from the bunker with his duffel bag.

"Let's get on the road, Lieutenant. I'll drive the first leg."

We jumped in the canvas-covered jeep. I rested my M16 on my lap, pointed to the right, and held Ott's rifle in a vertical position between the two seats. I looked over at Ott, wondering about his driving experience, wondering if he had the ability to guide the jeep in a fast escape or a quick stop.

The trip began in silence, the concern for survival obvious in the squint of our eyes. Our objective was to make it from the province's main artery to the principal north-south road that led to Saigon. We watched everywhere, our eyes and heads moving constantly, not wanting to die for the cause of a propane refrigerator.

Soon, however, we relaxed a little, lulled by the whine of the jeep's engine and the bouncing along the dirt road. The tedium of the drive and the tension of staying alert got to us. We both realized about the same moment that, every time we passed a couple of school girls on bikes or an old man with a wagon or a bus packed with local people, our survival was as much due to chance as to our readiness.

Ott broke the silence.

"The colonel said he didn't want to hear anything about this." Ott laughed. "Then he gave me the name of a restaurant in Saigon. He said it was the only place that hadn't gone downhill in his two tours here."

"That's a find, sir," I assured him. "I must have been to Saigon at least ten times, and the only place that is getting better is the USO on La Rue de Fleur. At least I know what their hamburgers are made of."

We talked on about such things, drifting into silence again, then chatting, then quiet.

"Paul, I never asked you about your family."

I told him about my family, the new generation of nephews and nieces. He told me about his.

"Those kids on the sampan…" Ott shook his head. "I can't help but wonder if they ever had any fun. I mean, my brother and I really had it made. We were army brats. We always had our mom trying to give us the best to make up for Dad being gone or the fact that we had to move about every two years to make the army happy. But, you know, we were happy. We liked each other, my brother and me. He's a doctor now. Couldn't stomach the army life. I was the one to carry on the family tradition."

"I know what you mean," I offered. "I was close to my brother and sister, I guess, like you. But I really liked my childhood. You know, if somebody asked me, 'Would you like your kids to grow up like you did? Would you choose that for them?' I guess I would."

"Right, I wouldn't have lived any other childhood. So, Paul, you ask yourself…you ask yourself about those kids. Why did they have to drown, and did they ever have a happy day in their lives?"

"You know, it's odd. I haven't seen that many crying kids over here. I mean, they all seem fairly happy, despite this war. When I was at Sa Dec, I did some teaching…" I paused, deciding about what to tell him of my Sa Dec days. "Of course, the older they get, the more serious they seem to get. But the ones I taught still seemed to smile and laugh just like any kid. I can't believe they're pretending. Maybe they're just finding the best in a bad situation. Maybe they don't know anything else."

"Yeah, maybe you're right. Maybe they do just think it's normal."

"Well, Major, I don't know. They gotta know that the war at its worst can do some damage to them. During Tet, I saw a baby who had a bullet in his gut from some Viet Cong. The nun at the hospital in Vinh Long told me that the VC shot him just because his father was an American."

Ott said nothing, concentrating on the road. He seemed to be looking for words. I think he was as distressed about the baby as he had been about the two kids in the sampan, maybe more. I think he wanted to convey some kind of understanding to me.

"Did you catch the guy who shot him?" he asked.

"We caught a few that day. But I guess I felt like somehow we had caused it as much as the VC did." I was thinking as I talked. "Major, I think maybe death is always like that. You know, you see a part of yourself die, too. I mean, the little boy I saw and the two kids yesterday…it's seeing innocence suffer and die, and it kills part of you, too."

Ott was silent in thought.

We approached a village, and both of us were back on guard. It was a small village and not particularly known as a haven for VC. But the people watched us as we watched them. It gave me a spooky sensation. We sped through the town, anxious to be out of it, slowing only for a water buffalo with a child on its back and for a bumbling bus. Outside the village, the miles passed with both of us lost in our own thoughts, streaking along the straight roads lined with trees and canals, more reminders of the French. We floated back into conversation.

"Paul, have you given any thought to death?"

The question surprised me.

"If you mean my own death, well…yes. I was completely preoccupied with it when I first got here. I thought about how I would change things if I got back to the States. At first, I thought about spending my life helping people. That baby I told you about…well, I would think about that baby and then decide I was going to go home and work with kids." I shook my head and shrugged. "But that's bullshit for me. I'm not patient enough. Anyway, that was my first thought.

"You know, before I got to Nam," I continued, "I figured that if I was told that I would only live for five months or some short time, I would play kamikaze and go after Castro or somebody else like that as if I were the chosen martyr to save the world!"

"You really have visions of grandeur, Lieutenant!" Ott teased.

I smiled in the embarrassment of my own candor.

"Then I had a sergeant who solved the whole thing for me. He was on his third mission in Nam, and I asked him one night how he had managed it and what he did when he left home. He told me he figured that the Lord looks down when he's ready for another one, and he picks the ones who have their lives in order, because the ones with all the problems are the ones who seem to survive. So he told me he left his life in total disarray based on that premise!"

"I like that!" Ott laughed again.

I kept talking, not really sure why.

"I sort of agree with the guy, sir. I mean, death seems prone to taking the best or the innocent. Like those kids. I had a classmate like that. He got through the best schools, married the best girl, was tops in our military intelligence class, got the best assignment in Saigon. Then I heard that he volunteered to go up in a gooney bird for a night operation. They were loaded with flares, and one of them prematurely ignited in the plane, sending all the other ones off. They say the plane was like a giant golden ball in the sky. Now, you have to wonder why that happened. Just a freak occurrence."

My meandering stopped, as we were becoming aware of sounds again. Ott slowed toward an intersection of roads as I craned my neck. It was a convoy of US military vehicles coming up the road. We turned onto a side road and waited, letting them all pass. The deuces, tow trucks, and jeeps passed by, and I offered to drive as we fell in behind them.

"No thanks, Lieutenant. I fall asleep if I don't drive. Just keep talking."

But the pace quickened now, the noise heightened, and the trucks kicked up dust clouds as we followed the convoy. I was back to watching the roadside. The road was far from the tree line, and the openness made me edgy, even though it was probably safer, since only a very good sniper would risk a shot.

We entered Saigon still behind the convoy, joining the mass of three-wheeled taxis, bicycles, buses, and pedestrians, all moving through the thick and constant smell of diesel fuel. I directed Ott away from the convoy toward the airfield. We passed the old racetrack where the VC had operated during Tet, now quiet and still, riddled with craters and burned-out buildings. We passed through the second of the guarded gates and drove down to the US Air Force supply depot. Ott pulled up on the gravel beside the building. It was a quiet area. Opposite the building were rows and rows of six-foot cubical boxes standing in the hot sun, looking not unlike a company of silent sentries. An occasional forklift vehicle emerged and moved down the line.

We entered the building and were greeted by a red-haired airman who sat behind a desk in a small, sweaty space with a noisy fan moving hot air. He humped to attention as he saw us.

"May I help you, sirs?"

"We're looking for Sergeant Winslow," I told him.

"He's out on a run to the Base Exchange, sir, but I think he'll be right back." The airman seemed a little puzzled, as though he wanted to inquire about why two army officers were in search of an air force staff sergeant.

"We'll wait outside," I told him. "By the way, have you got anything cold to drink, a Coke maybe?"

"Yes, sir, in the refrigerator. Costs a dime."

The airman pointed, and Ott and I walked over to the air-conditioned vault that contained the drinks. We would gladly have traded places with a Coke bottle at that point.

"I've got this one," Ott said, pulling out a dollar chit.

We stood outside the building in the shade, watching the activity, drinking, until Winslow drove up in a jeep. I waved him over to where we were standing.

"Lieutenant!" Winslow gave me a pimpled smile. "How you been, sir?" He looked just about like he had when he had served briefly at Sa Dec. He was overweight, his skin in a constant state of eruption, but he was always smiling. He had lost a stripe, I noted.

I did the introductions.

"I'm fine, Winslow. This is Major Ott. How'd you lose the stripe, Sergeant?"

"Long story, sir. I wish I was still back running the radio for the air force attachment." He spoke almost wistfully, then grinned again. "But this isn't bad duty. Anyway, what brings you up this way?"

Sa Dec had traded with Winslow before, and I came straight to the point.

"We've got five Chicoms. We need a propane refrigerator and a new stove…and some air conditioners."

Ott threw me a glance in surprise. It was the first he had heard about the air conditioners. But I knew Winslow, and I knew the bargaining had to be hard.

"What for, sir?" Winslow asked.

"Winslow, our team doesn't have anything to keep food in, and our stove is going out. Oh, and we need a generator for the air conditioners."

Ott was almost smiling now.

"Well, sir…" Winslow was going to spin out the bargaining process. "You see, the generators are all gone. And air conditioners are real hard to find. We don't even have one. I doubt if I could get you all that stuff for five Chicoms." He paused, frowning, and then he brightened. "But I have a stove and refrigerator. I can give you the electric one inside."

"Great, Winslow. But then we'll need the generator, too," I pushed.

"Yeah, you're right, Lieutenant. Maybe I can find a propane job. Put the rifles in my jeep. Come back tomorrow around ten a.m. I'll have your stuff and the forms."

We did as we were told. Ott jumped back in the jeep and settled himself again in the driver's seat.

"Can we trust him?" he asked as we drove off.

"We've got to, sir. He's the only guy I know who has access to stuff like this."

The rest of the day was a two-man rampage through the Base Exchange, followed by a couple of beers and spaghetti dinner at the officer's club, then back to a hotel.

"Next time," I promised Ott as we separated to go to our rooms, "I'll show you around. I have some friends in town, and I know a couple of great hotels. But it's been some time since I've been in Saigon, and I've never really been comfortable on the streets since Tet."

Ott did not disagree. He still showed the caution of his newness in country.

"No problem. This is just fine. All I want to do is get back. I don't want anyone to think we're on a joyride."

We had breakfast the next morning at the base officer's club: a real eggs-and-bacon buffet that was quite a treat. We made one more run to the Base Exchange for beer, M&Ms, of course, and cigarettes, and then drove back to the airfield.

As promised, Winslow was waiting for us. He was a bit nervous and spoke tersely.

"Bring your jeep over behind me," he instructed.

He drove the forklift, and we followed him in the jeep, down the long lines and isles of boxes, down to a particular container. He made short business of the lock on the container and opened it, revealing stoves packed in cardboard boxes. The three of us pulled out the first one and placed it in the trailer.

"The refers are over here," Winslow said in a hard whisper, pointing off to his right.

His nervousness was getting to Ott, and it had its effect on me, too. We worked quickly and with a little feverishness, loading on the refrigerator and tying both down on the little trailer.

"Listen, Lieutenant, if the guard stops you, just show him this paper," Winslow instructed. "But try not to get into a long conversation, and don't leave the paper."

We understood.

"Thanks, Winslow," I said as we finished the tie-down. "Hope you get that stripe back. And don't forget, you owe us an air conditioner and a generator."

"No way, sir!" Winslow looked upset. "That's all I can give you for five Chicoms!"

I smiled. I knew he was right, but I also knew Winslow. I was coming to know Ott, too. So I was not too surprised when he turned to me as Winslow departed.

"Paul, you want to drive?" He tone was nervous and a little excited. Once again, his interrogative was anything but a question. It was a request. I knew I was to drive.

We moved out of the supply depot and down toward the first gate. I held the papers high, and the guard glanced at them, seemingly satisfied. I drove toward the main entrance guard station, suddenly aware of the drag but not yet aware of the new dynamic dimensions that the loaded trailer added to the jeep.

As long as I drove in a fairly straight line, we were fine. But the moment I had to swerve slightly to make our way around a parked vehicle, the trailer took on a life of its own. Right and left, it fishtailed behind us. I speeded up, hoping to compensate, but not before the trailer, still careening, sideswiped a gray military bus that was moving in the opposite direction on our left. Ott and I could hear the sound of some brand-new creases being added to the side of the bus.

"Shit!" It was both of us speaking at the same moment. Ott lurched around in his seat to view the damage, and I slowed momentarily to do the same. At last I had the trailer under control, I thought. I saw the bus come to a stop and the driver now out of the vehicle chasing after us. I gunned the jeep's engine.

Ahead a half mile was the gatehouse.

"Major, if I stop, there'll be some tough questions!"

"Go for the gate, Pritchard!"

We did and at quite a clip. I could feel the trailer back in my control again, and with a glance in the mirror, I would see the Vietnamese bus driver still running after us.

The guard at the main gate was an American. I slowed down as we moved through the gate but stopped only on its other side, forcing the guard to look at us and not at the commotion of the yelling driver a quarter of a mile behind. I glanced back. The bus driver was still running, but the roar of the traffic on the busy main road drowned his yells. Ott was suddenly inspired. He stood up in the jeep, saluting the guard. That confused the guard for a moment and forced him to do the same.

"For Westmoreland's castle," I shouted to the guard, waving the papers.

"No problem, sir."

But I wasn't waiting to hear that. I was already pulling out and down the road. We stayed on the main roads, now lost and safer in the crowd of Saigon vehicles. I kept my eye on the mirror, knowing that the main roads were probably not the best idea, but not knowing any of the side roads to take. I half expected to see a military police jeep chasing us, but none appeared.

"Keep your eye out, Major; they may have called ahead to the MPs."

"Right!" Ott responded, again on the lookout. "By the way, Lieutenant, what the hell was that Westmoreland stuff?"

"It was the best I could do on short notice, sir. Anyway, don't you think Westmoreland ought to come out and visit us?"

We both laughed.

"I think you just saved my career, Lieutenant."

"Not yet, sir! Keep your eye out!"

We did. And I realized that I hadn't driven for almost a year.

Dear Mom and Dad,

Well, Dad, with another birthday over with, I'd just like to send my best thoughts for your future birthdays.

When I was younger, I thought we had all the problems in the world. But with the time at college, the experience meeting other families and seeing the way they responded to one another, I began to realize how fortunate we three kids have been to have such fine parents.

Once I remember I was trying to think of what one quality each of you has contributed to my life. My conclusion at the time was that you, Dad, gave me a sense of idealism, of dreaming but of putting it into the dimensions of reality. Mom gave me a sense of realism, of evaluating, judging objectively all the elements that surround me. Of course, each has done more.

Probably much more could be said about the love and the appreciation you have shown me. I am very grateful for all that you both have given me. I only hope I can take these innate qualities and put them into successful living.

Just a short "birthday card" to say I love you.

Paul

CHAPTER 13

❧

Turkeys are hard to find in Asia, but the US Army delivered that year in time for Thanksgiving. We cut the deal as the helicopter landed with the bird: I would prepare the turkey; Bellamy would handle the rest of the preparations; Ott and Wooten got the cleanup assignment. Dinner would consist of turkey (though we did have a canned roast beef backup), mashed potatoes from a box, cranberries in a can, and green beans in another number ten can. No one complained. It was as good as we could expect, and that was sufficient cause for giving thanks.

I had another cause for giving thanks. I had survived uncountable days and nights in Operation Phoenix. Now I would be home by Christmas. I had received those blessed words in writing that I was "rotating back" to the States. Since it was Christmastime, the army had thrown in a few more days to get me to Kansas City on time. I was going back on the fifteenth of December.

It was also something I kept to myself. You never knew who might get his nose bent out of shape at another's good fortune.

I was, though, in exceptionally good spirits as I cooked the turkey. Bellamy and I were cheerfully getting in each other's way as our preparations went on. Wooten's beer was safely tucked in the new refrigerator, and I had gotten into the bourbon I had brought back from the now-famous trip to Saigon.

"You know, Sarge,"—I waved the spoon I had just used to baste the bird—"the real heroes of this war are the supply guys. Intelligence keeps on screwing up, and everyone else at headquarters is a day late and a decision short, but I'll tell you, supply is on top of this war."

I closed the door of the precious, hard-won oven. "Think of it, Sarge. What do you suppose this bird cost?"

"I dunno." Bellamy paused his whipping of potatoes to think about it.

"Well, first, they send some guy out to a farmer in Alabama to buy a million turkeys for Vietnam. Then they wrap and pack them for shipment. So far, it's just like the one my family is eating right now." I stepped around the table, concentrating on this calculation, whipping the paper-dried spoon in my right hand.

"But then," I continued, "the US Army packs them up on a ship, or if I know them, on a plane, and wings them over to Nam. And imagine if that plane goes down. Think of the headlines: 'Military plane down in Pacific, stuffed with frozen turkeys.' Imagine the congressional investigation."

I was enjoying this. Bellamy smiled.

"Anyway, then they take them off the plane at Tan Son Nhut and put them back into storage. All the time, there's military guards, electricity for the generators, inspectors checking for spoilage. Then they pack them in small containers and fly them all over the goddamn countryside! And it's all for the boys, and I love it!"

"I got no complaints, Lieutenant," Bellamy said. "As long as I'm over here fighting for my country, I figure it's the least they can do. But, you know, Lieutenant…" Bellamy looked up at me with a hopeful smile. "You know, they might have some leftover turkeys. How about another trip to Saigon? Wooten and I could do it. I'd be happy to drive this time."

Ott, of course, had told and retold the story of our escape from the airfield.

"No way, Sarge." I laughed. "It's a delicate mission. If I know you two, you'd get caught and court martialed. You two would be the turkeys."

We continued in a companionable silence, the smell of the roasting turkey filling the bunker every time I opened the oven to check on it. I checked on it often, not even minding the waves of heat. I had read the instructions as I started this operation and had started poking around the bunker, searching for a paper bag. My mother, I remembered, had always put her turkeys in a brown paper grocery bag. Bellamy's mother apparently did things differently. He was astonished when I asked him if we had a paper sack around.

"I think it keeps the moisture in," I had explained to him. "Have we got one?"

He didn't think so.

"What the hell, I'll just keep basting it." I gave up my search. "I've got nothing better to do. With the time I've got left, I don't plan to leave this place."

A door opened behind me. Ott entered the bunker.

"When do we eat, Lieutenant?" he asked, meaning it literally. "We have to be at Gò Công by 0700 hours tomorrow. I want to get to bed early."

"We'll be on time, sir. Chow at five," I replied. Military time was seldom used by anyone but Ott, who probably thought career officers had to.

With Ott's reminder, the bunker was suddenly silent, full of the war again. I decided that the turkey could cook on its own for a few minutes and walked outside. The low, rain-laden clouds covered the sky, as they always did at this time of year. I watched them thoughtfully: the clouds, above it all; the sky, always the source of helicopter rescue; the clouds, the only place where you could blot out the war, where the sweat finally cooled you down. Rain clouds were welcome back in the parched Kansas summers of my youth.

It wasn't just the clouds; it wasn't just Thanksgiving, and it wasn't just the short time. Maybe it was all of it together. But I sensed myself already heading home.

I had been in Saigon enough. I had long forgotten Moi, Sa Dec, Tet, my past. And I was starting to take seriously the dedicated letters from Libba. I pulled out her latest.

I read again her recent letter: "Have you noticed that you seem to take a lot of pictures of clouds?" she had written in response to a batch of pictures I had sent her. I hadn't realized it until she pointed it out. It probably did look odd from her perspective.

I had decided that I would stop sending pictures back. I found myself preoccupied and vaguely worried about her process of analyzing me. Of course, I analyzed every word of her letters to me, and, of course, her observations were seldom wrong. But I didn't like her telling me that this is what she was doing.

What a foundation for a relationship! I could even appreciate the irony of the message I was sending her: go ahead and analyze me; I do it, too; and I know you're doing it, but don't tell me you're doing it.

There was no question that I was starting to take her seriously, though I really knew her very little. We had met and dated for about a month while I was at Fort Holabird. She was a bright, well-educated, classic Southern beauty. She was one of a few sweethearts when I left for Nam, and my absence took its toll. But she was the only one who kept writing to me. The others had slowly fallen away.

Of course, it was mostly my fault that they did. I wasn't much of a correspondent. When it came to writing letters, it was about all I could do to get regular notes off to the family in my cramped, left-handed script or wait until the next typewriter. So they stopped writing. They were all gone now, except for Libba.

"Lieutenant, how's the turkey?" Bellamy yelled, a subtle suggestion that I return.

Our Thanksgiving dinner was a great success. Everyone pushed thoughts of the morning out of their heads for a time and ate, drank, and told stories.

The next morning was a dismal anticlimax. Ott, Bellamy, and I got up at six to drive to the headquarters at Gò Công. We were tense. We seldom left the castle bunker at that time of the morning but were tightly alert for an ambush. We watched, ready.

As we pulled into the compound, I could see Lister. He was moving fast, trotting across the veranda of his house and down the steps, two at a time. He spotted us.

"We gotta see the chief!" he called out. "Lieutenant, come on with me."

"Take the jeep, Lieutenant." Ott hopped out, making room for Lister. "I've got a briefing."

Bellamy, Lister, and I headed through the early-morning hustle of people preparing for the day, through the town, past the shops to a section of old French colonial residences. The province chief's residence was like the others, with the plaster garden wall embedded with sharp shards of glass on the top. Guards watched over the entrance and the side drive. A stable of jeeps waited on the inside, always at the ready for the chief.

Lister leaped out of the jeep. Sergeant Bellamy tapped my shoulder and tossed me a small package.

"Here, Lieutenant. Take these. They're for the chief."

Bellamy was a good man, a pro. It was a pack of Salem cigarettes. He knew the chief liked them; he knew I didn't smoke often; and he knew my offering them to the chief would be well received.

"Thanks, Sarge," I said with a grateful smile. "Next time I go to Saigon, you go, too."

Lister was already at the door, and I had to run to catch up with him. We were met by a uniformed ARVN sergeant, who showed us in.

"The colonel will see you now. Please follow me."

The house was dark and cool despite the muggy morning outside. We followed the sergeant down a large center hall to a set of twin French doors on the left. He opened them silently, and we stepped into what had once been a dining room, a graceful sweep of a room, very European.

Now, however, it was an office. The province chief sat behind a large desk, a strong light shining in a pool over part of its surface. He seemed preoccupied. He didn't lift his eyes from the papers on his desk, and the visual message was unmistakable to me: "I'm a busy man. I will inconvenience myself for you, but do not keep me away from my work for long."

"Please have a seat." He looked up for a moment and waved us to the two chairs placed before his desk, then looked back down and continued his study of the papers. It seemed a long minute or maybe two before he looked up again.

"What is it that I can do for you?" he offered, finally.

"Colonel, thank you for taking the time to see us," began Lister in a tone that amazed me. His normally clipped and aggressive manner was gone.

"We are here, Colonel, in the hope that you will change your mind about the operation to capture General Chow."

I was all ears. And I was pissed. So this was the guy. And he was a general! Despite the fact that he was the target and my purpose for being where I was, Lister had never referred to him by name or rank.

"Colonel," Lister continued, "we realize that there is some risk to your men if we pursue him into the Rung Sat. But we believe that there is a good chance that we will catch him and some of his men if we strike now. Now, Colonel, right now." Lister emphasized his urgency. "I know that you told our colonel that"—he paused, probably to edit his words—"that you are not willing to support our operation at this time. But it is the US government's position that it is the best opportunity—we have the best opportunity right now."

There was silence. The colonel looked at us. He seemed for that moment to be peering across some vast space, over centuries of culture, a millennium of instinct. His eyes seemed to be searching for something.

It was my moment.

"May I offer you a cigarette, sir?" I asked, breaking the silence.

The colonel seemed pleased. He smiled, breaking the tension.

"Merci, Lieutenant."

I passed him the new pack and took one when the colonel offered them back to me. Lister declined. I handed them back.

"Please keep them, sir."

Silence returned as the colonel lighted his own and then, reaching across the desk, lighted my cigarette. We inhaled, and I think we both savored the diversion of the moment.

The colonel moved back in his chair, arranging himself, it seemed. "I do not understand you Americans," he said quietly. "You come here and tell us that you are our allies. You tell us that you are here to help us win our battle. You tell us that we must make the decisions. You tell us that we must make the decisions by your standards and procedures."

Lister shifted in his chair as the colonel paused, bringing his body forward in the chair.

"Then," he continued, his voice rising just slightly, "you contradict every decision we make."

The room felt suddenly cold. I had the uncomfortable feeling that Bellamy's cigarettes had kept us from being thrown out of the room. But they had not kept the colonel from releasing his frustration with Lister.

"It is your decision. If you wish to find Chow, I will not stop you from trying. But I will not risk the lives of my men. Show the Americans out, Sergeant."

I knew, as we left in silence, following the sergeant, that we were lucky to still be in our boots. I wondered if Lister realized it.

He didn't.

"Let's get Chow!" Lister's words were harsh as we walked back to the jeep, where Bellamy was waiting for us.

"Mr. Lister, with all due respect," I said, appalled at the bravado, "you do realize, don't you, that we have a problem here. I mean, if we do get Chow, we embarrass the colonel. If we don't, we lose face."

"Shit, Lieutenant!" Lister exploded. "We're here to win a goddamn war, not worry about some chicken shit colonel!"

Bellamy's eyes met mine. Thanksgiving was definitely over.

Lister was leaping out of the jeep even before it came to a stop at the compound. "You go get Dwain," he ordered. "I'm going to tell the colonel that we've got ourselves a mission. An hour, Pritchard. I want you guys ready in an hour." And he was gone.

I left Bellamy with the jeep and walked up the familiar steps and into the house that Lister occupied. Dwain was in his room, sitting at the desk when I entered. He seemed to be contemplating something, a photograph, I thought, and he was lost in another and distant reality.

"Lister wants us ready to go in an hour."

"What for?" Dwain looked up and over at me but did not move from his chair. We had grown no closer than the first meeting.

"The province chief went along with the mission."

"Is he giving us any backup?"

"No."

"Fuck!" Dwain's words and body seemed to explode at once. He was up and pacing around the room, distracted. "Fuck! This is a goddamn disaster in the making! What the fuck are we doing?"

I stepped back to avoid collision with him. Dwain stormed off down the hall. I followed, wondering what came next.

Lister was coming across the parking area as Dwain and I emerged from the house. Dwain was still charging, and Lister read it perfectly.

"Goddammit, Dwain, we can hit this guy!" Lister wasn't waiting for the question.

Dwain and I stopped. Lister moved in close to Dwain, looking spindly and odd against the huge bulk of Dwain. "Get this straight. I make the decisions here. Not you. The mission is on."

Dwain stayed right where he was, right in Lister's face, his chest heaving for a moment under his cutoff sweatshirt. "Fuck, man! Can't you see this is a setup? And if it's not and we don't have ARVN behind us, we're out there by ourselves! By ourselves! Fuck!"

Lister didn't move either, but he waved his arms.

"Shit, yes, I realize that! Maybe that's good! Maybe we'll show the goddamn ARVN that we're here to win a war! I've got the best helicopters coming in: gunships, Cobras, the whole nine yards! Look, Dwain, I'm going for a touchdown! Now get ready!"

Dwain was silenced. It was my turn.

"Lister, what did our guy say? Did he OK this?"

Lister whirled toward me, his eyes flashing.

"Look, Pritchard, I don't need his or anybody else's OK. He's gone. We are going out. I run this program, and that's my decision."

Lister started to stalk off toward the house, then stopped. Turning back to us, he had a full head of steam now. "Goddammit!" He shouted across the veranda, "I want Chow! And you guys are going to go get him! And if you can't, I'll go do it myself! I call the shots in this province! Just get that straight! And get your goddamn men ready!"

I looked at Dwain.

"Our very own warlord," I began. Dwain and I realized at the same moment, I think, that we were in this together.

But Dwain was beyond communication of any kind. He had already started walking back to the house. I waited alone on the steps. I had just a few days before heading home and now the State Department needed a score, a fucking touchdown. Only, if we failed, we wouldn't just lose points. If we failed, no one would be there. No one would know. There was nobody in the stadium. And I might lose my ass.

Dear Brenda and the Gang,

    Talking about pets (you were, weren't you?), we have quite a menagerie here at the headquarters. We have a male and a female monkey, George and Georgette, who never cease to amaze me. Last night I found them romping around the front of the house. They climbed up on a jeep that some fellow had covered with his poncho, since canvas tops are hard to come by. Well, I would tap the inside of the top, where I could tell they were sitting. Then they would come tearing over after me and try to jump on my back before I was able to get out and away. You never really realize what exactly they're after till you feel your glasses whipped off your nose and watch them as they scamper up a tree. Then it's an hour of tempting and scolding till they finally come down and relinquish the now-chewed-up and lip-marked glasses.

    We also have a gecko here, a large lizard that hides in the vines on the house and occasionally screams out a strange two-syllable yell that sounds a little like his name. Lizards are everywhere over here. They scamper over the walls to eat the numerous mosquitos and insects. It's fascinating to watch them as they stalk a bug on the screen and then make it disappear before your very eyes.

    And a dog, too. I'm sure she is not as good as your Mr. Magoo, but she does have her own personality. For instance, she loves to play volleyball. She can't bounce it on her nose or anything like that, but she can keep it rolling like a soccer ball. I must admit that Mutsy has an ulterior motive in that her boyfriend lives near the volleyball court. So she'll play with us for a few minutes just to humor us and then sneak off to play with him.

The people over here have some different types of pets compared to ours. Their water buffalo, even though they use them to pull their plows and grow the rice, still are the perfect pet for the little children who take care of them, watch after them while resting on their backs, give them a bath, walk with them to a new job. You might think that the child is watching after the water buffalo, but the buffalo is also watching after the child, keeping him constantly busy and each of them benefiting. How's that for compatible?

On day last spring I was walking down a road, and I saw a boy standing on water and moving sideways at the same time. Yet he did not take a step. Then I saw the objects sticking out of the water ahead of him that made up the water buffalo's nostrils and eyes. His horns fell just below the water as he raised his nose to keep it in the air. The boy was standing on his back and getting a high-and-dry ride. I think I have some pictures that I took of it. Remind me to check when I get home.

So much for the pet-sy side of the war, huh? I hope that you all have a beautiful fall and that you can get out to see the colorful sights around you.

Let me know if I can get anything for you before I leave. I hope that I gave you an idea of what can be bought over here.

See you in a little while.

Short-Timer
Paul

CHAPTER 14

⚜

ANOTHER MISSION. HOW MANY HAD there been? I wondered. They all seemed to swirl around in my mind like mixing vanilla and chocolate in a bowl. Hopefully this was the last.

The jeep headed to the waiting choppers. I was still trying to get my mind around Lister. I hated this feeling. I was in the control of this man who represented an invisible force—the State Department. Worse, Lister was a driven man whose cause was more important, more consuming, than any other issue, cause, or life. That included mine.

Dwain was quiet, driving the jeep without a word. He seemed spent by his outburst and maybe by Lister's. In fact, he seemed quite unconcerned now, or maybe, like me, he was just numbed. I bargained with myself: *Come on, you've worried about missions before and come out without a scratch. Maybe this is the last big one, and you're out of this hellhole. Relax.*

The choppers were waiting along the roadside, attracting the attention of Vietnamese children who had run along the road to watch. It was a strange assortment of troop carriers, known as UH-1 Deltas, two Cobras, and a Bell observation chopper. Their blades were still rotating but in a more or less resting mode. My mercenary troops were called by radio and were already out of the ARVN half-ton trucks, mounting up as we arrived. They were quiet, too.

"I'm Major Raible." An American approached us. "I understand that one of you, a Mr. Lister, has the State Department's OK on this trip."

Lister stepped forward and started a reply, but the major cut him off.

"I just want you to know that this is one hell of a dangerous zone, Mr. Lister," the major said with emphasis. "Now, you've got the ships you want, but I'm not too happy about putting my men and my equipment out there in the Rung Sat."

Lister's face contorted for a second as though he were ready for another tirade; then it passed.

"I hear you, Major. Now let's get going."

Raible gave Lister a long look but said nothing. He turned to the line of choppers and gave a circling hand signal over his head that required no explanation. The Bell took off first, followed by the Cobra. The Deltas, complete with their Delta Airlines bumper stickers, waited until everyone was on board. It was a small joke here in the Mekong Delta, to say the least, but I noticed them.

My squad was already buckled in on the canvas seats when I hopped up. There were greetings from Bodai and the usual official smiles from the rest of them.

"Ou est le VC?" asked Bodai.

"Sais pas, mon ami. Nous allons a la Rung Sat," I replied.

Bodai's eyes narrowed, and he said nothing. Rung Sat, however, was all any of them needed to hear. It required no translation into any of the languages they spoke. They were silent. The roar of the engines and the blades precluded conversation anyway.

One of the pilots up front turned and signaled to me to put on the headset. "Lieutenant, this is your pilot speaking. It's a pleasure to have you fly Delta Airlines. This must be some kind of crack unit you got here." The voice was monotonously calm, accented, I thought, with some down-home Oklahoma.

"Roger, Captain. We are some sort of crack unit." I responded in the same monotone, keeping the sarcasm to myself.

The chopper lifted off, following the formation in front of us. I could see the Cobra, which was swinging off behind the formation. I stayed on the headset, listening.

"Major, let's keep close to the ground. And let's get there as fast as possible." It was a disembodied voice, crackling from the troop carrier directly behind mine. But it was definitely Lister.

"Roger, Mr. Lister," came Raible's reply.

We moved forward, slanted at an angle, with the nose of the ship pointed to the horizon. I was balancing myself and watching my squad do the same. My senses were inexpressibly sharp. I could smell the moist air and feel the atmospheric conditions change as the chopper plowed the air. I could smell the moisture of rice paddies and the JP-4 fuel. I was alternately drenched with sweat and then cooled as the chopper moved and the rush of air filled the cabin.

The pilot glanced back at me, catching my attention.

"You guys know what you're doing? This is one place we've never been." His voice was just the same as before.

"Roger. Piece of cake," I replied, still with sarcasm.

The pilot turned around to look at me again; this time his eyes searched mine to see if I meant that. I let him search for a moment, then averted his gaze. Outside, the countryside was right there. The chopper was barely a hundred feet above ground. It rose occasionally to avoid a tree row and charged on at what felt like about a hundred and fifty miles an hour. My squad members said nothing. Nothing to me, nothing to one another. No one moved. They all seemed to be someplace else.

The pilot turned to me again.

"Lieutenant," he began, his voice still calm. "Lieutenant, he can't hear you now. Is this guy Lister in charge?"

"Roger."

"Lieutenant, let me tell you, he really pulled some weight to get this mission OK'd. Shee-it! Everybody back at base was pissed off royal! You do realize that, Lieutenant?" The pilot's calm was gone.

"Roger."

I didn't know what else to say. I was still debating myself. Maybe this was the time to come clean with my feeling about this trip and just tell the pilots. Feeling? Bullshit! It was experience. My experience was better than Lister's. This chopper was full of experienced men who knew better than Lister. All I had to do was say something. Maybe they'd all agree. Maybe it would force Lister to order us back rather than have to explain a mutiny. A mutiny...

I was at about that place in my mind's debate when it was cut short.

"Mr. Lister." Raible's voice came over the headset. "We're going to spread out to cut down this noise." Raible, the consummate officer, was doing his duty.

The choppers began to spread out, taking a parallel formation.

"Lieutenant." It was the pilot again. "We're going to let our copilot here pick up some grass."

I looked up, amazed. But the pilot's back was facing me. The chopper dropped slowly without losing forward speed, and I caught sight of some reeds about three feet long stuck to the skids of the chopper. I watched these chopper jockeys with appreciation. They were just like me. Under someone else's control. Up on a mission put together by somebody else. Just waiting for the surprises, the disasters. Knowing only the coordinates of the drop zone and nothing more. So they made the best of it.

"Got it, ole boy," came the pilot's voice, "here we go."

The chopper rose quickly back to about a hundred feet, responding as though it wanted to put some distance between itself and the ground every bit as much as we did.

We moved over the river, a wide body of water with a few sampans quietly plying their course, then moving quickly toward the shore, hugging that shore, as the small armada above them moved overhead. The Rung Sat covered the horizon. As far as I could see in the morning sun, it was nothing but islands of small trees and silver ropes of water surrounding the mangrove. There were no roads, no rice fields, no visual landmarks, nothing.

"We're five minutes out," Raible announced. "Lock and load." His command was classic infantry, not chopperese. Not that we needed it. Everyone was already on the alert.

Suddenly, the chopper was taking hits. Lots of them.

"We're taking fire," said the pilot coolly. "No damage, Major."

I could feel the chopper's shift of motion. Though I couldn't see the gunners, they were firing away. I could see the Cobra, and it looked like it was moving on a target.

"Keep up, Snake!" It was Raible now on the headset. "We need you with us!"

The Cobra pulled out of its low firing position, then back with the rest of the choppers. We were coming in on the target. It was a large island, and there were several sampans with straight shaft motors. Each sampan had two men in black. The sampans broke into all directions at once.

"Forget the landing! Go for the boats!" Lister's shout came through the headset.

"We're just like ducks about to light, Lister. They can get us easy," came Raible's response.

"I said go for the goddamn boats!" Lister was screeching now. "We've got him! We've got Chow in one of those boats!"

Suddenly, there was heavy fire. It was coming from the island.

"Keep low! Avoid their fire! And go for the boats, goddammit!"

"OK, men." Raible's voice filled the headset with a calm and a competence. "Go for the nearest target, but keep within visual contact."

Raible's men knew their stuff. The choppers seemed to swing off in all directions without further coordination. The swing of the troop carrier was as heady as a kid on a swing, hanging on the edge of the arc before gravity pulled it back.

I could see a sampan pulling into the shadow of some trees below. Then we swung again. The headset was filled with the shouting chatter of the pilots and the cacophony of gunfire. When I saw the sampan again, the two men were firing back at us with automatics.

"We got our boat!" Lister yelled. "If you see any survivors, shoot them in the water."

There was a sudden and total silence on the headset.

"Dwain! Get ready! Get your men ready to go in!"

"Mr. Lister…" It was Raible. "You get this straight. There is no place to land, and we're not prepared with ropes. This place is infested with VC. We're heading back. I can't endanger my men anymore."

There was another moment of silence. It was clear that nobody except Lister could justify hanging around, shooting men in the water like ducks or being shot at like the landing ducks Raible had compared us to.

Lister's voice came back, full of excitement, almost gleeful, giddy, and half hysterical.

"I'm positive we got Chow! He looked just like the guy!"

"Roger, Mr. Lister, whatever you say," Raible replied patiently.

I breathed for the first time in several minutes as the showdown ended. It was a deep breath of relief. I filled my lungs with the moist air as we pulled away, feeling a kind of exhilaration.

It was altogether premature.

The plinking sound of hits came out of nowhere and enveloped the chopper. Blood shot out and across the cabin. It was coming from the man sitting nearest the door, coming from his arm. I reached toward him instinctively to help, but in that instant I was knocked back into the cavity of the cabin with the weight of Bodai. Dead. Blood gushed from his chest, drenching me as he slumped toward me, held in place only by his seatbelt.

"Goddammit!" I screamed to no one. To everyone.

The pilot was on the headset again, talking to the door gunners. There was one voice in reply where there should have been two. The pilot turned in my direction, signaling but not looking. I loosened my seatbelt, shifted the load of the dead man, and looked back. Still strapped in was the dead door gunner. There was a mosaic of bullet holes concentrated around him.

I fell back across the open area and shook my head slowly at the pilot. Then, with my headset back on, I reported.

"We've got two dead and one seriously wounded. Goddammit, Lister, do you hear me?"

"I hear you, Lieutenant. Keep your cool," came Lister's reply.

"Cool, fuck! We've got two dead. You tell them to keep their cool!" Raible cut in.

"We're going straight to My Tho. Who got hit?"

"It's Baker, Major," came the pilot's voice.

"Anybody else take any rounds or got any wounded?" Raible asked.

There was silence.

"OK, men. Let's get into My Tho. Chuck, watch your oil. Watch your gauges. One of those rounds might have hit your engine or the lines. Keep low in case you lose control. We'll follow you."

"Roger, we'll get her to My Tho."

I looked back at the cabin. Bodai had stopped profusely bleeding, but there was a huge pool now, dark red and deepening, covering the corrugated floor. The wounded man sat with his head against the engine housing. He grimaced and whimpered softly.

"How you doin', Lieutenant?" the pilot asked.

I had to check. I knew I felt nothing but the M16, warm from having been fired in the frenzy. I looked down at my bloody torso and had to consciously take inventory to assure myself that the torso was mine, but the blood was Bodai's.

"I'm OK."

CHAPTER 15

⚜

THE BEGINNING AND END WERE really much the same.

I had received my orders to report for processing out of country. I had the obligatory farewell party at the castle bunker and then flew to Saigon for more goodbyes there. The comings and goings of Americans, soldiers rotating back, were hardly uncommon. Everyone was used to this kind of thing.

I had expected a debriefing when I got to Saigon or at least some kind of discussion, but there was none. In fact, the only mark of interest, ceremonial or otherwise, was the demand that I turn in my duffel bag of gear, which was mostly unused during my tour. Handing back my M16 was different, sort of like parting with a friend but more like parting with a dependency. I had already passed on the derringer to Ott and the 9 mm pistol to Bellamy back at the castle. I wondered if drug addicts felt like that when they parted with their last needle, the symbol of so much past and what they want not to have in the future.

"Report with your gear to the bus, men. Your plane will depart in two hours." The sergeant stood before the group of us, moving quickly, checking names on a clipboard.

"Shit, Sarge, you think anybody's going to miss this? You think anyone wants to stay around for more?" It was the voice of one of the sixty GIs with whom I stood.

The laughter was genuine. I couldn't tell which of the men had said it, but it didn't matter. Any one of us, officer, enlisted, or NCO, could have said the same thing.

I boarded the plane, a regular Boeing commercial aviation craft, just like the one I had taken to Nam. The crew of stewardesses were dressed in the same uniforms as on the flight over. But there was a difference. All of us did an amazing amount of gawking. The women, the food, and the movie: it all struck me as unreal, surreal, not possible. A Disneyland for the mind after a year of killing and stopping the killing, of fatigue and tension.

"Do you think they'll have a big parade for us when we land?" my seat-mate asked. I wasn't sure if he was serious.

"I don't know," I replied. "Probably not. But, you know, it's funny. I never really thought about it until now."

"Yeah," he seemed to muse, "I've probably seen too many war movies."

I knew what he meant. As I answered him, I had a black-and-white motion picture in my head, straight out of World War II movies, with tickertape and parades and dockside beauties kissing every GI who got off the board.

"Jensen." He announced his name, offering his hand.

"Pritchard." I shook it.

"What did you do in Nam, Pritchard?"

I told him my story, or at least as much of it as I felt like talking about.

"What about you?" I asked.

"I was in supply. Up north. Two Corps. You'd think they could have found some better use for a master's in finance, but it was keeping track of jeep parts for me. At least I got a lot of reading done."

I was starting to like this guy—another misplaced soul who made the best of it.

"Jensen, tell me something. Were you guys winning up north?" I asked.

"Hell, I never knew." He settled back in his seat. "I mean, I just listened to the numbers for the first few days I was in country. Then I realized that if you multiplied the KIAs reported by our provinces, we would wipe out the entire population in just under five years. I stopped paying attention. There was just so much bullshit."

"I know what you mean. I sometimes think this whole war was a lie."

"Think?" Jensen was getting engaged now. "Think, hell! Of course it was a lie. It was a game, a numbers game. It was like letting the New York Jets keep their own score without a referee! Shit, if the fans knew the coach could just claim any score, they'd demand a victory every game. And that's what we were up to. Congress wanted a victory, and, by God, that's what we gave them."

I was surprised at his candor and by the depth of his frustration, even though I agreed with him.

"So you think there was nothing of value going on there, Jensen?"

"Value is a funny word, especially for a finance grad," he responded. "Value for anything is what you want it to be. My watch may have great value to me and little or none to you."

"Yeah, I know. I guess I meant something else. I mean, do you think we had any legitimate reason for being there?"

"I wouldn't use the word 'legitimate' either, my friend." Jensen paused, thoughtful for a moment. "I know what you mean. I used to ask myself that all the time. But you have to remember that I wasn't out there in the war, like you were, to see it for real."

"That's OK, Jensen," I encouraged him. "I can handle it. What did you decide?"

"Well, I decided that war is the ultimate numbers game. I mean, the objective is to determine how much your side is willing to lose for something else, for whatever it is that the other side has. How much, my friend? Now, each item you're losing has value to society. The life of a GI is worth something to Americans; the life of a VC, very little. But I wouldn't want to say that one GI's life is worth more to his family than one VC's to his family."

Jensen was taking on an academic tone, looking at me like a captive audience. The pictures sprang full blown into my mind, the two drowned children whose price quieted the parents, the nun handing me the baby. I wondered if he could make sense of the reality.

"There are other things, other values to be considered." He was midsentence when I caught up with his speech. "On the mundane level, there is the value of having a trained and experienced military."

"You mean that this war is a training camp?" I asked.

"Well?" he replied.

I knew he wasn't that far off. He pursued the point.

"Don't you think so? Didn't you see some of that?"

"Yeah, I saw career guys getting their combat experience. But you can't think that the war was about training officers!"

"I don't know, my friend. I'm not judging the purposes, now. I'm just identifying them."

He was right in a way.

"New weapons, new machinery, all the paraphernalia…" I was thinking out loud.

"Now, you're on my wavelength!" He was exultant and ready to go on. "Then we have to add in a trained intelligence apparatus, you know, the old State Department, your old boss. This was their testing ground, if you ask me."

"But what about the politics of it, Jensen? I mean the historical aspect of this war. That shit."

"Listen, Pritchard. I once wanted to go into divinity school until I realized that life is a game of odds, not serving causes. Birth is a case of the odds; living to the age of sixteen is a case of the odds; then from sixteen to twenty-one, it's another set of odds, and so on. Ask the warrior guys. War just increases the odds against survival. I don't buy this lofty purpose crap. Hell, the American Revolution was started because a king forgot about the numbers, the amount of tax he could charge and get by with it. The Civil War was a battle over the numbers: property and capital. There were slave owners in the north, too, you know."

Jensen was getting on my nerves with his pedantry. He could tell.

"Face it, man. History is an expression of numbers and their relationship to one another. It's not values, and it's certainly not legitimacy." He stopped.

We passed the rest of the flight in silence, broken occasionally with what my father would have called idle prattle. We walked off the plane together and into a cool San Francisco day, brisk and bright. There was no band, no flags, no one to greet us but the military police.

"Do you have any drugs, weapons, or illegal items to declare?"

I swallowed those words of welcome. Jensen stood behind me in the long line of duffel bag–laden men as we filed into the processing room.

"I guess they forgot we were coming."

"Right, Jensen," I said with a smile. "Wonder what the odds were that they'd remember?"

There was a clerk waiting at the travel desk, ready with tickets, and then another bus ride to the San Francisco airport. There was some irony in all this sudden army efficiency. Every GI wanted it and probably would have chosen it. *Forget the ceremonies of thanks, guys. Just get me out that door*, I concluded.

Once at the airport, some headed immediately for the restrooms to change into street clothes and trash the fatigues. We didn't really talk much.

But one man, still dazed it seemed, perhaps spoke for most of us when he told the whole bus: "Christ! I fired off my last clip into a bunch of VC, dropped my rifle, turned around, and here I am. What a war!"

I had a little more time to get used to things than the men who lived in California. I was headed home via Dallas, and the flights and the waiting gave me breathing time to sweep the Disneyland sensation away.

There were three of us waiting in Dallas for the flight. The desk steward had summoned us to the counter and now looked at us with a stony, flat expression.

"Men, I'm sorry. The plane is full. We're going to hold you until the end in case we have a no-show. Otherwise, we'll get you on the next flight in five hours."

"I can't wait here," lamented one of the men. "My family's driving in from the farm. They're already on their way!"

The desk steward's expression didn't change.

We loitered around the counter, watching the minutes tick away on the wall clock, checking for the appearance of any late arrivers. One came. With no more than a minute or two before scheduled departure, the steward announced that there was room for two of us.

"Put these two men on. I'll wait." It was my last act as an officer, and I wanted to remember myself as a gentleman, I kidded. Actually, all I had to do was telephone to tell them I would be late. And I found that I wasn't really in that much of a hurry.

"Let me close up the ship here," the steward offered, walking down the ramp. "And then we'll find another flight for you."

He returned, bustling, followed by a middle-aged man dressed in a dark business suit.

"This must be your lucky day," he said. "You just got this man's seat in first class."

"Why?"

"Ask him."

The man was waiting for me as I turned away from the counter.

"Thank you, sir," I said, reaching to shake his proffered hand. "Are you sure you want to give it up?"

"Least I can do, Lieutenant. I want you to know I appreciate what you've done for us. It's a small token."

I was choked for a moment. Here was somebody who didn't live by the numbers.

"Thank you, sir. Thank you very much." I turned to head down the ramp to the waiting plane.

"Lieutenant," the man said softly, behind me. I turned back.

"Merry Christmas, Lieutenant."

Printed in Great Britain
by Amazon